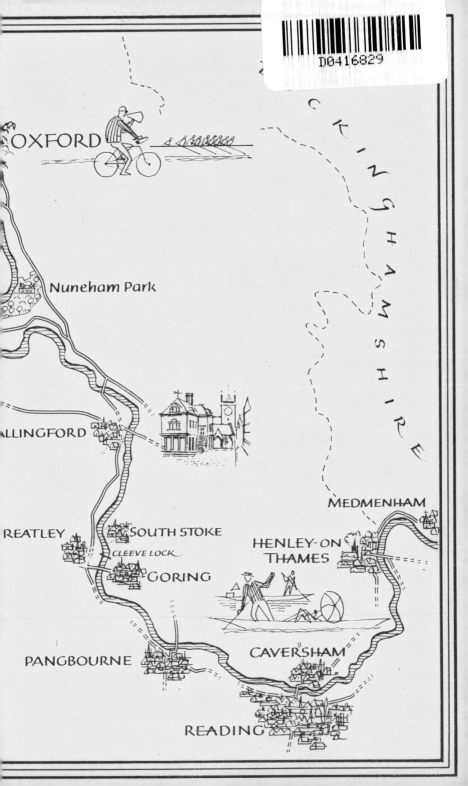

An Eye on the Thames

Books by Alan Wykes

Novels

PURSUIT TILL MORNING

THE MUSIC SLEEPING

THE PEN FRIEND

HAPPYLAND

Literature

A CONCISE SURVEY OF AMERICAN LITERATURE

Collaborations

with Lord Brabazon of Tara: THE BRABAZON STORY
with J. A. Hunter: HUNTER'S TRACKS
with Captain Wilfred H. Scott-Shawe: MARINER'S TALE
with D. A. Rayner: THE GREAT YACHT RACE

Profiles

SNAKE MAN

NIMROD SMITH

THE DOCTOR AND HIS ENEMY

AN EYE ON THE THAMES

Anthology

A SEX BY THEMSELVES: comic drawings about women

Entertainment

PARTY GAMES

AMATEUR DRAMATICS

Sociology

GAMBLING: a Definitive Study

An Eye on the Thames

ALAN WYKES

JARROLDS

JARROLDS PUBLISHERS (LONDON) LTD
178–202 Great Portland Street, London W1

AN IMPRINT OF THE   HUTCHINSON GROUP

London Melbourne Sydney
Auckland Bombay Toronto
Johannesburg New York

First published 1966

*This book has been set in Baskerville, printed in Great Britain
on Antique Wove paper by Anchor Press, and
bound by Wm. Brendon, both of Tiptree, Essex*

to
JOHN WORSLEY
artist

Acknowledgements

My thanks to J. Watson Parton, Honorary Secretary of the River Thames Society; Herbert W. Cremer, C.B.E.; Local Government Officers of the Thames towns and cities mentioned herein; and the Information Officers of the Thames Conservancy and the Port of London Authority.

*

The extract from *The Historic Thames* by Hilaire Belloc is printed by permission of A. D. Peters & Co.; from *The City in History* by Lewis Mumford by permission of the publishers, Martin Secker & Warburg Ltd; from *History of England* by G. M. Trevelyan by permission of the publishers, Longmans, Green & Co. Ltd; from *Zuleika Dobson* by Max Beerbohm by permission of the publishers The Bodley Head Ltd; from *Three Men In a Boat* by Jerome K. Jerome by permission of the publishers, J. M. Dent & Sons Ltd, and the Executrix of the Jerome K. Jerome Estate; from *The Departmental Committee's Report on the Pollution of the Tidal Thames* by permission of the Director of Publications of Her Majesty's Stationery Office; from *Shades of Eton* by Percy Lubbock by permission of the publishers, Jonathan Cape Ltd, and the Executors of the Percy Lubbock Estate. The stanza from Poem 32 in *The Magnetic Mountain*, from *Collected Poems 1954*, by Cecil Day Lewis, is printed by permission of Mr Day Lewis and his publishers, The Hogarth Press Ltd and Jonathan Cape Ltd.

Contents

Illustrations

I

A Mort of Potamologists

I

READING, Berkshire, where I live (though I am not a Redin-gensian), is an overcrowded industrial town of, at the time of writing, some hundred and twenty-five thousand people. The building of the M4 motorway has brought London within a possible forty minutes' fast driving—always assuming you can extricate yourself from the traffic muddles of the town centre and strike the motorway before you are shrivelled to a bunch of frustrations—and this possibility has encouraged a great many industrialists to hive their offices and factories off from London's great wen and attach them to Reading's smaller one; so the great and the small will soon be joined by the car-cinoma of twentieth-century conurbation.

The town is administratively half-baked, artistically null, and, apart from a very few vistas of decrepit but otherwise pleasing eighteenth-century houses, architecturally hideous. (Even that enthusiastic proponent of Victorian design Mr John Betjeman is said to have blenched and asked for a res-torative glass on seeing the town hall for the first time.) Histor-ically, though, Reading is of some importance and a curious burrower through its archives will find matters of interest. The importance, and through it the interest, derives from the town's location at the confluence of two rivers, the Kennet and the Thames—a site doubtless chosen by the original settlers for reasons common to the choice of all riverside settle-ments: for the presence of water and, consequently, game and fish for food; and for security in defence.

My own house is in a road running more or less parallel with the Thames—which of course flows from west to east across most of the southern half of England. The house is a couple of miles up the south side of the river valley, which continues its rise opposite my front door across a hundred and twenty acres of public parkland to the summit of the valley and beyond that to the main London to Bath road. Beyond that the ground slopes smoothly down again to the Kennet, which joins the Thames about three miles to the east just within the town boundary. The park was until recent years the home of a rich merchant, and his house—a somewhat grim structure vaguely Italianate in style—stands on the summit I've just mentioned, between the two river valleys, facing south across the levelly turfed slope down to the Bath Road, but with its view beyond that obstructed by eight-storey blocks of flats.

Only a few years ago I could stand on the terrace of the mansion and look south across miles of pastureland into the neighbouring county, Hampshire, and gain an aesthetic satisfaction from the design ordered by geology and husbandry; now, according to mood, I can loose arrows of splenetic thought at the flats, or—more reasonably—stretch my meditations into a far more distant past. I can conjecture, for example, on the mood of some Roman legionary standing on guard in his cantonment where the mansion now is and gazing the other way, northward across the Thames valley. I can also guess at his thoughts had he been granted a precognitive sight of the very un-Roman terrace of villas in which I live. Though seventeen or eighteen centuries divide us in time his reaction is likely to have been as cross as mine at having his view obstructed; and no doubt he would have murmured—as a great many people have murmured since Horace murmured it first—'Alas, the fleeting years are slipping by'. Fortunately the fleeting years have left their mark— and only in rocks have they left it more ineradicably than in the conduits along which rivers flow through the land. True, six hundred million years have slipped by since the shuddering upheavals of the Proterozoic ages began the formation of the terraqueous globe we live on, and for only the last ten thousand of them has the world's landscape settled down to the shape we know today; but ten thousand years offer quite a field of exploration for several studies—geology, hydrology, and anthropology for instance, plus, much nearer this end of those ten thousand years, the recorded history of people. Absorbing studies all, but too vast in measure for any one student in his lifetime. One must define, narrow the field down. And this is easiest done at the dictates of temperament and circumstance. My own temperament inclines me to look at people first and at the earth they live in second. But which people, which bit of the earth? Circumstance has eased me into position : I live in the Thames valley, I have only to walk a couple of miles down the valley side and I come to the river. My question is answered : I can look at the Thames and some of the people who, performing the antics of history, have been on it or in it, who have been pleased by it, frustrated by it, saved by it, or despatched by it. There are more than enough of them and, at my time of life, there's more than enough distance to cover, comparatively short though the river is.

Indeed, the Thames is the shortest famous river in the world. Its two hundred and ten miles are linearly insignificant compared with the Nile's four thousand one hundred and sixty; its strength, measured by the disasters it has caused, is puny compared with the Mississippi's. The Ganges is holier; the Don is swampier; the Danube is by repute bluer; the Loire is certainly prettier. But comparisons, between rivers as between people, are in themselves unimportant. Besides, the origin of all rivers—as distinct from their visible 'sources'— is common : they are a consequence of the precipitation of the water in the earth's atmosphere. This falls as rain, hail, snow, sleet and mist, and either evaporates directly back into the atmosphere (a process hastened by the heat of the sun), runs off hills and mountains (a process delayed by frost and ice), or is absorbed by the soil. Of that which is absorbed by the soil some will evaporate after return to the surface by capillary action or transpiration by plant life, the rest will sink deeper underground into the rocks forming the earth's crust. At places where the rocks can contain no more, the water will be forced to the surface again through fissures and will seep out as springs. So, as you see, the formation of the earth's rocky crust, and the distribution of its mountains, determine the sources of all rivers: they either issue from the depths or run off the peaks. And the contours of the earth's surface determine their courses to the sea. But they are common in origin in the sense of all being links in the circulation of the hydrosphere. In the general scheme of things the Amazon is no more important than the Bain, in Yorkshire, which is only a mile or so long. And that, in a way, neatly cuts the Amazon down to size. But specific rivers, like specific houses, flowers, typewriters, photographs, chairs, mothers-in-law, curates, tea-pots, cats, popes, buses, and the centillion and one other things that make up life in general, have specific importance for the people who have to do with them. I don't feel I have to find any more procreant reason for looking at the Thames.

Although I live on its valley side I cannot see the river without going down to its very banks. Houses and fences and trees get in the way; also the undulations of the ground, for, unlike the slope down from the far side of the mansion in the park, the ground behind my house is not at all even—in fact at the end of the garden it slopes up instead of down and this knoll is dotted with bungalows. But a walk of a few hundred yards along the road to the east brings me to a gap in the houses where, on a fine day, there is a good view of the valley (though the river itself remains invisible) right across to a corresponding height on its far side. That side is Oxfordshire and the sight of it is a lot prettier than the reverse view across to this bit of Berkshire. It is that vista, as much as anything, that has charmed me into thinking of the Thames valley and the river itself as 'mine'. I have never wanted to adopt Reading (any more, probably, than it has wanted to adopt me), but it has, as you see, proved to be a convenient launching point for this essay in potamography.

II

The study of rivers has occupied a mort of potamologists and potamographers down the ages. Some of them have simply recorded what other eyes and ears have seen and heard; others have gone about their studies and descriptions the hard way; others still have blinded us with science. In the first category one would include Pliny, that charming but gullible historian of natural phenomena, who notes that 'There is a river in Bithynia called Olachas, running close into Briazus (which is the name both of a temple and also of the god therein honoured) the water whereof will discover and detect a perjured person : for if he that drinketh thereof, feel (as it were) a burning fire within his body, take him for a false forsworn villain. Furthermore, in Cantabria or Biscay the fountains of the river Tamaricus, are endued with a secret virtue to presage and foretell future events. . . . In Iurie there is a river which every Sabbath day is dry.'

Those who have looked and studied for themselves and have endured much in the looking include of course all the intrepid explorers of the mighty rivers like the Nile and the Amazon; but they include also men who have submerged themselves in diving gear to measure pressures so that the strength of embankments could be calculated, or to study the formation of river beds so that tunnels beneath them could be planned. Some of the science-blinders have presented us with formulae for measuring the volume of water discharged into a river basin in a specified time, some have formed themselves into teams to produce reports for such bodies as the Water Pollution Research Board, some have studied rivers for their algae, or their contentiousness in matters of boundary law, or

B

their potentialities as sources of hydro-electric power. Whatever they have done it seems doubtful if in the doing of it many of them have called themselves potamologists. But that is what they are.

Such a mass of scientific and historical facts about rivers is on record that even to choose from those concerning a specific river like the Thames is a hard job. But a reporter cannot do better than begin at the beginning. There are of course two beginnings to every river—one in time and one in space; but as it is beyond me to establish when the Thames was first forced out of the earth by the circumstance of the Gloucestershire rocks having reached their absorption limit, I shall content myself with a look at its spatial origin.

This is easy enough. Unlike Herodotus pursuing the course of the Nile in the fifth century B.C. and being forced to turn back at Assnan because of the waterfall there and the lack of information on what lay beyond, I can get to the source of the Thames without trouble—an easy three days on foot, a couple of hours by train. Herodotus reported: 'No-one can speak about the source of the Nile. Concerning its course I have now told all I could learn by enquiry. It issues into Egypt: this is all I shall say concerning the Nile.' And indeed two thousand three hundred years passed before anyone could say much more. But even England's earliest backwoodsmen needn't have puzzled long about the source of the Thames. As Hilaire Belloc points out in *The Historic Thames*, 'From the beginning of human activity in this island the whole length of the river has been set with human settlements never far removed from one another; for the Thames ran through the heart of South England, and wherever its banks were secure from recurrent floods it furnished those who settled on them with three main things which every early village requires: good water, defence, and communication.'

Since finding the source of the Thames poses no problem I went to look at it very early in the course of my researches for this book. This was to be a preliminary look only. I planned to travel the whole length of the river either on its surface

or its banks—sometimes both. But the source seemed to me
the place that would warrant the extra attention that would
get me in perfect tune with my subject—which I already
thought of possessively as 'my' river, you recall. So I pried
myself away from my desk and boarded a train to Kemble, a
Gloucestershire village only a mile or so from Thames Head.

III

Fifteen hundred million gallons of water fall over the weir at
Teddington—less than two hundred miles from Thames
Head—most days. One readily understands that the source of
a river can be a mere trickle, and that it is the continual pressure urging the trickle from the ground that builds it up into
the enormous volume that accumulates towards the mouth.
One understands too that numerous tributaries feed the
main river, and that with such an element as water it is impossible to attribute any specific percentages of those fifteen
hundred million gallons to the main and tributary rivers.
But if one were able to skim off every pint that had come from
the tributaries and found that only a third of the fifteen hundred
million gallons came from the main river's source, it would
still be astonishing to consider the contrast between the volume of water at Teddington and that at Thames Head.
Personally I was astonished to the point of incredulity : for no
water at all issues from the designated source of the Thames.

This source is an alleged Roman well beside an ash tree
on which someone has cut the letters T.H. There is no positive
evidence of the Roman origin of the well, and not much of
its being a well at all. There are a few stones in circular
formation, but they enclose only more stones in a small heap.
As for the initials of the words Thames Head on the tree, the
bark has now healed to such an extent that they are almost
as invisible as the water one reasonably expects to find at the
source of a river; but they are there, though they may not

mean what they are supposed to mean. Tradition perpetuates fallacy as often as it perpetuates fact. It is possible that
the initials are the initials of some lover once briefly here in
assignation and convinced that the event was worth pub-
licising; it is possible that the ring of stones was assembled
here by some long-dead canny showman wanting to exploit
the gullibility of simple travellers willing to pay to touch dry
but allegedly 'holy' wells. It is also possible that the source is
altogether elsewhere. Many people have been saying for
centuries that the true source is the Seven Springs pool, about
fourteen miles to the north, just outside the town of Cheltenham; and indeed one of them has felt so strongly about it that
he has gone to the trouble of saying so in Latin and cutting
an inscription in a tablet at the pool: '*Hic tuus O Tamisine
Pater septemgeminus fons*' ('Here, O Father Thames, is
your sevenfold fount'). But this is the source of another river,
the Churn, which joins the Thames some miles to the south-
east, *after* the Thames has become a sizeable stream. Other
supposed—and, indeed, possible—sources are the springs of
two other tributary rivers, the Coln and the Leach, both of
which rise a little higher in the hills and join the Thames
even farther downstream than Cricklade, which is a good
eight miles from Thames Head.

(I may say that I had acquired this smattering of knowledge, and was even prepared to be suitably astonished at the
lack of water at Thames Head, before I entrained for
Kemble. In an enterprise of this kind I like to arm myself
with the facts, select those that seem interesting and relevant,
add my own interpretations and observations, and conjure
the whole into a coherent picture which I hope someone may
look over my shoulder at.)

Personally, I am willing to go along with tradition regarding
Thames Head, in spite of there being no visible water there
when I looked at it this first time. There is, as I was to see
later, a seepage out of the ground, if not out of the supposed
well, during winter; and even on this day in a dry summer
there was some not far away across a couple of fields. The

area around Thames Head is called The Mede (more accurately Trewsbury Mede, since it is part of the grounds of Trewsbury House)—an archaic form of the word meadow, which includes among its meanings 'a tract of moist grassland along a watercourse'—and to my mind there's very little doubt, scientific or otherwise, that the watercourse in question is the Thames. So far as I could discover, the doubts cast on Thames Head being the true source originated with a sixteenth-century potamologist who visited the place and too readily accepted the evidence of his own eyes: there was no water there at the time, *ergo* this wasn't the source. The man's name was Walter Shipton, and what he says (in a pamphlet called *Anatomie of Tamesis*) is, 'No water floweth hereabouts til Leche, the true begettor.' But Shipton was a friend of Michael Drayton, the pastoral poet who wrote a long poem called *Polyolbion*, all about England's historical glories and topographical beauties, and they both had a great affection for their youthful stamping ground 'the lively Leche' (as Drayton calls it) which Shipton was understandably anxious to perpetuate.

Anyway, assuming that Thames Head is the head of the Thames, I'd like to quote another observer—not a potamologist this time but a Member of Parliament. This was John Burns, the first working man ever to become a cabinet minister, who was born in 1858 and died in 1943. Sometime between these two dates he was entertaining two Americans to tea on the terrace of the House of Commons. The talk had been of rivers and it had been fairly boastful on the Americans' part. Burns evidently thought the time had come for some comment about the river that flowed past the terrace. 'Gentlemen,' he said, 'the Saint Lawrence is cold muddy water; the Mississippi is warm muddy water; but this 'ere Thames is liquid 'istory.' In the circumstances his chauvinism can be forgiven.

All rivers are of course liquid history. Liquid pre-history too. And a brief consideration of what is known about the pre-history of the Thames won't come amiss here.

Britain was once part of the mainland of Europe. Measured by geological time this was comparatively recently—something between ten and twenty thousand years ago. After well over six hundred million years of structural alterations the earth was entering the Holocene[1] epoch. The ice age was ending. Glaciers which for a million years had covered the land masses of Europe and America were melting and the continents we know began to emerge from the seas of liquefying ice, the hollows in the land's surface forming basins to contain the lakes that are there today. Britain emerged from the melting ice as a promontory of northern Europe, the North Sea having already been formed as the result of the subsidence of land beneath it during the Pliocene epoch some ten million years earlier. (The Atlantic had been formed earlier still—probably about seventy million years ago—as the result of volcanic activity during the Eocene epoch.) A subsidence similar to that resulting in the North Sea was to cause the formation of a channel—the English Channel—across the southern end of the promontory towards the end of the ice age. But for the time being Britain was a spiky bit of Europe projecting northward. The Thames was in those days geologically noteworthy for two reasons : it formed across the promontory the southern demarcation line of arctic glaciers; and it flowed on eastward across the land that joined Britain with the Netherlands, Belgium, and France (as they now are) and formed a confluence with the Rhine at a point approximately midway between Harwich and Amsterdam. There the two rivers flowed northward in a single widening channel until they poured into the North Sea about a hundred miles east of what is now the coast of Norfolk.

None of this geological information is to any great extent conjectural. Geologists are not much given to conjecture : they base their science on facts and tell us what the facts mean as illuminated by the light of their knowledge. They may argue among themselves about, for instance, the time spanned

1. In the International Scientific Vocabulary Holocene means 'recent'.

by the Ordovician epoch, but their explanations to the lay-
man of the geology of the earth are always acceptable and
for the most part incontrovertible. If they tell us—as they
have—that fossilised sea creatures have been found on the
summits of Himalayan mountains, and that those mountains
consist largely of limestone which could have had its origin
only in the sea, it is easy to accept their fact-backed explanation that the mountains, seas, deserts, and canyons that we
know are the products of a six-hundred-million-year geological evolution that has raised the mountains from the seas,
dried the seas into deserts, and volcanised rocks into ocean
beds and Grand Canyons. So it is no great trouble to clearly
visualise a Thames that was longer than the one we know
and which—probably as recently as fifteen thousand years ago
—was a wallowing place for hippopotamuses and a water
source for lions. The geological facts to prove it are on record.

Man, such as he then was, had migrated radially from
Africa, learning on the long journey—it was long both geographically and generically—to hunt lesser creatures, and
kill them for food. He also learnt to use rivers for his own
benefit. There is plenty of archaeological evidence to prove
that he'd come upon the Thames well back in what we often
call the Stone Age—that is, towards the end of the Pleistocene
epoch, when he'd developed enough skill to make himself
tools and weapons of stone. (This was about two hundred
thousand years ago.) The discovery of such tools in the
Thames valley is one of the proofs that Britain was joined
to the mainland of Europe, since without boats—which man
didn't invent until he was relatively civilised—he couldn't
have crossed deep water. His natural fear of the unknown
would have prevented him attempting to swim unless he
could have seen land on the far side. (The suggestion put
forward by some Doubting Thomases that those ancient tools
were part of the collection of some Celtic or Roman archaeologist doesn't bear examination: they have been dug up
along almost the entire length of the Thames, which is too

widely dispersed an area for any archaeologist to lose or scatter his collection in; and even the Doubting Thomases don't suggest that there were dozens of ancient archaeologists living on the river banks and continually burying their treasures with intent to deceive future generations.)

The Thames would of course have presented to prehistoric man the same problems and the same uses that other rivers had presented during his radial explorations from his place of origin—which we assume to be Africa until evidence to suggest otherwise crops up. The hundreds of generations that successively extended their wanderings across the earth must slowly have learnt that rivers supplied that necessity of existence, water, that they didn't define the limits of exploration, that they could be forded where shallow and narrow, and that they formed a line of defence where deep and wide.

The story of Britain as an island naturally doesn't begin until it irrevocably became one, which was about seven thousand years ago, when civilisation was well on the march; and the story of the Thames doesn't begin to be interesting until people began to record its effect on their lives. But I think it will be helpful to sketch in a background of the island Britain as it was in, say, the fifth century B.C.—which is a time not too remote to grasp, when people were living lives recognisably similar to, although less elaborate than, ours.

IV

The people who organised the habitable parts of pre-Roman Britain into communities recognisably similar to today's were the Celts. They were tall, fair people with long heads and they came from what is now Germany. Much given to exploration, even when it involved battle and conquest, they spread out to Catalonia, Spain, France, Transylvania, and Anatolia. Though they were of common stock they quarrelled fiercely among themselves, developed tribal dialects, and adopted distinctive customs. But when they had a common cause they abandoned their bickerings and demonstrated unity. If the common cause was conquest they assembled in their chariots into battle formation brandishing their bronze and iron swords and pressed vigorously on to the boundaries of the people to be conquered.

In Britain, these were the Iberians, a Caucasoid race descended from the Mauretanians of northern Africa. The Iberians had spread from the European peninsula of Spain, Portugal, and the Basque region of the Pyrenees, and had gone into Britain when it was still joined to Europe. They too had long heads, but the hair on them was dark and their bodies were stocky. Also, their temperament was different. They had little feeling for commerce; and their explorations were nomadic rather than vigorous and curious, as were the Celts'. They were probably quite cheerful when the waters flooded across the lower end of the lush forested area they had discovered in their wanderings and cut them off from what is now France. No doubt it was about then that the now well known English characteristic of insularity began to develop. But the Iberians were no dimwits: they had some knowledge of agriculture and were skilled in engineering, metal working, military architecture (as shown by their earthworks), and several other useful accomplishments.

The English Channel having isolated them from the mainland, and the mountains of Wales and Scotland from whatever lay beyond to the west and north, they pitched their tribal camps in the southern and eastern parts of the territory and settled down temporarily but contentedly like cats in warm corners. These earliest settlers must have been unaware that they were inhabiting an island. Their migrations across Europe had been north-westerly, leading them eventually up through the corner of Britain we now call Kent until they were halted by the marshlands of the lower reaches of the Thames—which, you recall, until recently (in a geological sense) had been gushing on eastward into the Rhine and was now gushing instead into the inundations made by the North Sea. Thus halted, they spread westward through what are now Surrey, Sussex, Hampshire, Berkshire, Wiltshire, and Gloucestershire, to discover that the river in its middle and upper reaches no longer impeded their north-westerly wanderings and that there was a lot more land to be explored and exploited on the far side of the fordable places. These timid pererrations would have taken successive generations north into the midlands and east into the fen counties, and eventually as far up as the Pennines and as far west as the Welsh mountains. But since the country north of the Thames was far more forbidding and far less cultivable than that south of it the concentration of habitation was for centuries in the lower end of Britain. There the Iberians dug out their cosy corners (literally, for they lived in pits) and prepared for what with them passed for permanent settlement, only very gradually experimenting in travels northward to find again and again that they were stopped by mountain ranges or impenetrable forests from discovering what lay beyond and that the line of least resistance offered by settlement in the south really suited them very well. Even if they concentrated in this end of the country there was still plenty of space to be nomadic in.

This peaceful but relatively unprogressive state of affairs had been cocooning the Iberians for probably several thousand years before the Celts arrived in their lowboats and galleys, bent on invasion and conquest. But if I give the impression that the Celts were the first foreigners to arrive after the separation of Britain from the mainland I must correct this at once. There had been a continual commerce with Egyptian, Mediterranean, and Levantine traders—certainly from 2500 B.C. and probably long before. These merchants had found the island rich in metals (including alluvial gold) and pearls, and had paid for them, in part, by disseminating the influences of the earliest European and Egyptian civilisations. It is quite probable too that there were sporadic invasions of a colonising, rather than a commercial, nature long before the first Celts arrived around 600 B.C. But such invasions must have been repelled by the Iberians—who, if not enthusiastic about territorial expansion, were never wanting when it came to upping and defending the country they'd wandered into and had subsequently found sealed off by the English Channel. Potential invaders may have been repelled also by the weather, which then as now was changeable, and the increasingly difficult terrain north of the Thames. So foreign visitors were for the most part business men who overcame the natives' indifference to commerce often enough to establish firm trading associations. Island or not, Britain was in no sense isolated from the splendours of early civilisation by the time of the first Celtic conquest.

This conquest was by a branch of the Celts called the Gaels, who, as a result of the internecine strife I've mentioned as being characteristic of the race, had developed their own language. Uniting their tribes in the common cause of conquest the Gaels attacked Britain along its southern shore. There are no written records of the attack, only archaeological ones, but you may safely assume that they came in hordes and that their enthusiasm and superior knowledge of the techniques of attack were too much for the inherent peacefulness and purely defensive tactics of the Iberians, who were gradually driven north and west to take refuge in the mountains. Not so very long after this invasion—perhaps a hundred years—another horde of Celts attacked Britain and established the conquest more firmly than ever. These were the tribes united under the Celtic branch names of Brythons and Cymri. Again, though racially of common stock with the Gaels, they had developed languages of their own and were much more closely related to the Gauls than to the Gaelic Celts. The long term result of these two Celtic conquests was fourfold: the Iberians were driven farther and farther west and north into Ireland and Scotland, where the influence of the Gaelic language is still obvious today; the Cymri left a similarly conspicuous linguistic influence on the Iberians they drove into Wales; the Brythons gave their language to Cornwall (into which peninsula they drove the Iberians they found in what are now Hampshire and Dorset), and their name, in modified form, to Britain; and the genetic combination of the Celtic and Iberian races formed a strain that is the basis of British blood today—though it was later corrupted, if that is the word, by the genetic peculiarities of invading Saxons, Angles, Jutes, Danes, and Normans.

Although, as a consequence of their truck with foreign traders, the Iberians had acquired the several skills I have mentioned, the opportunities to exercise them were limited. The densely forested hills and undrained marshes of the lower levels damped their limited enthusiasm for economic agriculture; metal work was confined mainly to making hunting weapons, and engineering to the raising of such ritualistic monuments as Stonehenge. Six centuries before Christ the inhabitants of Britain—which at that time had no name and seems to have been referred to by merchants and invaders earlier than the Celts as 'the isle of tin'—were probably engaged mainly in hunting wild pigs, building mud and wattle huts and pits for living and storing grain in, and excavating tombs for the ritual burying of the dead (there are plenty of these 'barrows' to be seen today). Their social order was similar to the conquering Celts' own, if less advanced. It was the order of the clan or tribe, with chieftains ruling only their own small units of society. So there was no need for the Celts to make sweeping changes. As conquerors they were probably merciful. No doubt they exacted heavy taxes in the form of sheep, oxen, horses, and serfs; and ritualistic sacrifices to pagan gods would naturally be drawn from the ranks of the conquered. But such scanty evidence as there is suggests only that the Celts were lovers of the art of war, not that they were pathologically brutal.

The Brythonic Celts had greater knowledge of agriculture than had the Gaelic ones; they were also religious maniacs, their caste of priests, the Druids, being complete despots in that they ordered the punishment of death for disobedience of any of their complex theological rules. The Gaels had a simpler faith that was not dependent on hundreds of human sacrifices (in which the death agonies of the victims were interpreted by the priests as a divine language), but, rather, on principles of humility. They dedicated woods and forests as temples of worship and entered them submissively, bound hand and foot and dragging themselves over the ground until they exhausted themselves and presumably extirpated their sins. Between them, then, the several branches of Celtic invaders brought opposing religions, great organising ability, agricultural knowledge, and the power to strengthen the tribal system of living in which chiefs were only acknowledged heads and leaders and had no feudal or territorial rights. That system prevailed until the later conquests of the Saxon kings.

It was the Celtic organising ability, plus Brythonic confidence in agriculture, that resulted in the community life recognisably similar to today's that I mentioned a few pages back. The Celts had invaded 'the isle of tin' to find a familiar social structure that needed only injections of enthusiasm to keep it going and a land that (anyway at its southern end) was ideal for agricultural development. They had neither the nous nor the skill in agriculture that the later Saxons had, but they at least recognised the potentialities of the land and they put under the plough much of it that had for centuries been lush but untended. The natural result of their recognition was the establishment of villages of dwellings for the workers that were of a much more permanent nature than the pits and wattle shelters of the Iberians, who rarely put down roots and moved on elsewhere as soon as natural hazards or inconveniences revealed themselves.

In *The City In History* Lewis Mumford remarks that the agricultural revolution in Britain would have been almost impossible if it had been left to a nomadic people (like the Iberians): 'It needed something like the permanent occupation of an area, prolonged enough to follow the whole cycle of growth, to prompt primitive folk to have an insight into natural processes and to duplicate them more systematically.

Perhaps the central event in this whole development was the domestication of man himself.'

With that swift glance at pre-historic Britain to fill in the background I can now continue following the course of the Thames, which is what I set out to do.

2

Celts and Christians

I

THE Celtic conquerors had about five hundred years to establish their way of life before the next lot of invaders, the
Romans, arrived to establish theirs. Having no central government, the Celts fought as separate tribes for what they wanted,
whether it was good hunting country, agricultural land, or
earth with rich deposits of metal in it. The tribes who had
won the Thames valley and held dominant positions throughout its length were the Dobunni at the source end of the river,
the Catuvellauni and the Atrebates north and south res-
pectively of its middle reaches, and the Trinovantes and
Cantii north and south of the estuary. Of these, the Catuvellauni were the most powerful, and in Chapter 3 I shall peer
into the effect of the mid-reaches of the Thames on the Catu-
vellaunian battles. Here, my concern is with the Dobunni and
their battles with the Roman invaders near the river's source.

The Cotswold area of Gloucestershire had attracted even
the earliest Iberian settlers. Its light soil and the absence of
dense forest must have seemed ideal to wanderers who had
traversed the marshier regions to the east. And its lush pastures were doubtless well populated with sheep. (The sheep
have diminished in numbers but the lush pasturage remains.
The seventeenth-century writer Thomas Fuller says that he
has 'heard it reported from credible persons, that such the
fruitfulness of the [Cotswold] land, that in spring time, let
it be bit bare to the roots, a wand [sapling] laid along therein

overnight will be covered with new-grown grass by the next morning'.)

The defensive advantages of the high ground and the domestic potentialities of the soil, plus the easy availability of fresh water from the Thames and its headstreams, must have made the Cotswolds a worthwhile prize to the Romans when they came. They came for the first time, you may remember, under the leadership of Julius Caesar in 55 B.C. But that invasion was unsuccessful (Julius pushed his small army no more than ten miles inland from Dover). So was his next, a year later, when he brought the famed Tenth Legion. But on that occasion he penetrated deeper, fording the Thames at Lud, the Celtic settlement that stood where London stands today, and battling on into Catuvellauni territory in Hertfordshire. I say 'battling on' advisedly. Suetonius, a gossipy and unreliable writer, says that Julius 'invaded Britain, a hitherto unknown country,[1] and defeated the natives, from whom he exacted a large sum of money as well as hostages for future good behaviour'. G. M. Trevelyan, who was a true historian and a great deal more reliable, points out that Julius 'won several battles and penetrated into the . . . territory of Cassivelaunus, King of the Catuvellauni. That tribe was dominant in southern Britain and the jealousies caused by its hegemony turned some of its rivals and subjects into allies of the Roman invader. . . . But many of the Britons, including the men of Kent, put up a stout fight against Caesar, and though their undisciplined infantry were useless against the "legion's ordered line", the yellow-haired, athletic aristocracy of the Celts in their scythed chariots clattered down the warways of the battle like heroes of Homer, in a manner disconcerting even to veterans of the Tenth. The chariot, however, had seen its day as a method of warfare; it had already been abandoned in Celtic Gaul . . . and the British Chiefs would have been more truly formidable if they had taught themselves to fight as cavalry. . . . The expedition of 54 B.C., though not a failure like that of the year before, was no great

1. Nonsense.

success . . . the famous British Gold was secured in very inadequate quantities; the slaves were too ignorant to fetch fancy
prices in the market, and there had been neither the time nor
the means to carry off rebellious clans wholesale to the
auctioneer, as was Caesar's practice in Gaul. The expedition
had no permanent results, except as a memory on both sides
of the channel.'

It is, as you see, clear from Trevelyan (as it is from Haver-
field and other historians of the Roman occupation of Britain)
that Julius did not defeat Britain. A later Caesar, however,
did—though only in a military sense. That was Tiberius
Claudius Drusus—shortly, Claudius—a man of poor health
and suspected mental deficiency who was far from being any
great shakes as a soldier but met very little resistance in the
early stages of his invasion because many of the English tribal
chiefs had developed even stronger Roman sympathies as a
result of the increasing domination of the Catuvellauni. There
was, as it were, a Fifth Column that had paved the way between Julius's abortive attempt and Claudius's successful one
in A.D. 43. (Not that the Roman legionaries had things all
their own way : the later bitter resistance of Queen Boadicea
and her tribe of Iceni in A.D. 61 was an example of the strong
element of antipathy to Roman rule.)

Claudius appointed an experienced soldier and admini-
strator, Aulus Plautius, to lead the invasion, and Aulus and
his five legions of soldiery had virtually completed conquest
of the lowlands in the east by A.D. 47, when Aulus was
appointed governor to the imperial province of Britain, since
it was by then reasonably certain that the whole island could
be subjugated. Scotland, of course, never was, and Hadrian's
wall marking the frontier marked also an admission of over-
confidence. But Wales and northern England, with their
rich deposits of iron, gold, and lead, were firmly in Roman
hands by A.D. 84. (Subjugation, of course, does not necessarily mean successful colonisation; and in the sense of leaving
a permanent influence on British civilisation the Romans failed
completely in their conquest.) Broadly, the Roman method

c

of warfare was to surround an area with forts and roads, subjugate the surrounded natives, and then withdraw the best fighting troops and leave the defence of the area to local militia garrisoned in a fortified town. High ground has great military value in any encircling tactics, and the Cotswolds were of particular importance in establishing the two fortified Roman towns of Corinium (Cirencester) and Glevum Colonia (Gloucester). These were on sites selected by Ostorius Scapula, the Governor of Britain who succeeded Aulus Plautius, pushed the frontier of Roman occupation diagonally westward across England to a line (marked today by the Fosse Way) stretching from Lincoln in the north-east to Exeter in the south-west, and then fought on into Wales against the stubborn tribe of Silures. Corinium was especially valuable strategically because it made a convenient focal point for the Fosse Way and the roads from Verulamium (St Albans) and Calleva (Silchester), both of which were Celtic tribal capitals. The Dobunni were as well aware of the strategic value of the crossing site as was Ostorius Scapula. They were prepared to fight for it, and did.

II

The Dobunni were a Brythonic tribe. They were fierce in mien and colourful in their dress (as were all the Gaulish Celts). They wore brilliantly parti-coloured tunics checkered like the tabards of knights of medieval times, encircled their necks and arms with gold chains, and blue-rinsed their blond hair with woad. Both men and women, old and young, fought in defence of tribal territory. A Roman officer under Ostorius wrote of them : 'They are . . . terrible in the fierceness of their eyes, greedy of quarrels, bragging and insolent. A band of strangers could not resist one of them in a brawl, assisted by his strong, blue-eyed wife, especially when she begins—gnashing her teeth, her neck swollen, brandishing her vast and snowy arms, and kicking her heels at the same time—to

deliver her fisticuffs, like bolts from the twisted strings of a
catapult. The voices of many are threatening and formidable.
They are quick to anger but quickly appeased. All are clean
in their persons; nor among them is ever seen any man or
woman squalid in ragged garments.'

According to the evidence there was a Dobunni village at
Cricklade (eight miles downstream from Thames Head, you
remember). It was probably built on timber platforms sup-
ported by piles driven into the river bed—a common form of
construction where the ground was marshy and the river
needed defending because it was fordable. From here the
Dobunni would have had their first sight of the Roman advance troops approaching from the east. To convey the news
up to the chief's headquarters on the prized high ground
above the spot we now call Thames Head would have taken
no more than a few hours—a few minutes if a smoke signal
was used. The general summons to battle followed. Formations of chariots and cavalry were mustered. The women
abandoned their housewifery and the men unsheathed their
swords. Small working parties of the militarily incompetent
were charged with looking to the river's defences—wickedly
pointed stakes, both along the banks and submerged beneath
the water itself, so that fording horses had their bellies impaled as they attempted the crossing.

Tactically, the Dobunni onslaught was wasteful. As Trevelyan noted, the Celts were undisciplined and relied on noise,
courage, and numbers for their effects. The Romans of
Ostorius had gained considerable experience of Celtic on-
slaughts during their battles from east to west across England.
Some of them fell beneath the scythes fixed to the Celtic
chariots and the swords and spears brandished by the ill-
trained cavalry, but their lives were only temporarily dis-
arrayed. They advanced towards Cricklade relentlessly, their
discipline and cunning in deploying their forces being a good
match for the uncontrolled fury of the Dobunni. Their aim
with the *pilum*, a long-shafted iron-headed spear, was very

accurate and they aimed at the horses since the chariots, however wicked the mowing down power of their scythes, were
useless when immobilised. Robbed of their vehicles and engaged in close combat the Dobunni gave no quarter. Yelling
their battle cries they laid about them with axe and short-
sword; but many of their blows fell uselessly on the Romans'
superior armour. Never retreating, they either fell where
they fought or hacked off the unarmoured legs of the
Roman cavalry and impaled the underparts of the plunging
horses on spears or gashed them across their jugular veins
with axes. That Roman officer who remarked their furious
character said that, 'At the end of the day we had advanced
over their dead to the marshy overflow of the narrow Tamesis. In the light of our fires it was impossible to distinguish
between pools of blood and water. A limb, rigid in death, rose
from the waterweeds, a decapitated head could be seen among
the rushes. Everywhere was chaos of men and horses and
chariots. The Dobunni are not orderly fighters. We had
driven through them and they had spilled down the sides of
our columns instead of retreating and reorganising their
defences. They were altogether on the wrong side of Tamesis,
their defence line. They had sped to the attack without thinking, and now they had given us the advantage.'

However, the river was to reverse the advantage for a
while. Recorded history is vague about the season, but evidently the battle for Thames Head was fought in one of England's innumerable wet spells. The Churn, coming down from
the hill on which Corinium was to be built, joined the Thames
at Cricklade and the undrained land at the junction collected
rainwater from the surrounding hills as well. The surrounding
medes were waterlogged, the course of the river difficult to
determine except where the Dobunni's pointed stakes marked
the banks where it flowed beneath the raised village. The
Roman legionaries rounded up the Dobunni who had tactically played into their hands, moved north-east and south-west
to higher ground, and incarcerated their prisoners in palis-
aded enclosures. They then prepared to skirt the flooded

meadows and move on to their objective. Preparation, however, was dependent on supplies coming forward from the rear. Since many of their battles against the Catuvellauni and much of their progress through the country spanning the middle reaches of the Thames had been hampered by quaggy land, they had learnt by experience that supplies were best transported by river; otherwise the commissariat was liable to be delayed by being forced to take circuitous routes to avoid getting bogged down. The supplies were packed into the holds of flat-bottomed, square-sailed barges which were towed or rowed, as occasion demanded, by prisoner-of-war slaves (and sometimes by elephants, toys of war whose value the Romans had learnt, at considerable cost to themselves, from the Carthaginians in 218 B.C.). Supply points could be established wherever the river offered substantial banks; supplies were then taken forward from there to the fighting troops by wagon.

This system had worked well all the way up river from Wallingford (or thereabouts), where there had been some bitter fighting against the Atrebates, who held the south bank of the river in strength and had starved out a thousand legionaries by ambushing their overland supply trains. There seemed to be no reason why it shouldn't work now. While up on the hill at the Thames Head the Dobunni mustered more men for another attack, the Romans dug themselves in in fortified positions and waited for their supply barges to catch them up.

They had to wait some days. River transport was slow and was made even slower by the many changes in water level, which necessitated manhandling the barges up and down ramps. But at last the supplies reached Lechlade, eight miles downstream from Cricklade. Here again is a confluence of rivers, the Leche joining the Thames; but in those days the junction was not distinguishable in the shallow lake bordered by marsh that covered a hundred or so acres of undrained land at Lechlade. Nor was the course of the river. It was impossible to navigate accurately. The barges simply ran off course and grounded, each having tried to outdo the one ahead in navigational skill. There was nothing to be done now but unload all the supplies and tote them the eight miles to Cricklade. This, however, was less easily done than said. The water was shallow enough to ground the heavily loaded barges, but it was too deep to be forded by heavily loaded slaves, who also sank into the mud with their sacks of grain. There was an abundance of expendable slaves but no surplus of stores. A human chain passing the stuff from barge to dry land was tried, but many of the slaves forming the chain were sucked down into the bog and the stores irretrievably lost. The only answer was to drive piles down and build a bridge across. This took several more days. The garrison at Cricklade with its large complement of horses was being considerably reduced in efficiency by lack of food. The attack on Thames Head was also being delayed, and the delay was giving the Dobunni every opportunity to muster more men from Cotswold villages to the north and west. They had learned their lesson in the abortive attack on the Roman column and had decided this time to defend the high ground instead of foolhardily attacking the fortifications at Cricklade, though had they known of the Romans' lack of supplies they might well have successfully wiped out best part of a legion. But by the time the bridge was built and men and horses fed and restored two weeks had passed and the Dobunni had assembled themselves in great numbers behind earth fortifications in the area round Thames Head.

The hill was not impregnable, but it took a lot more capturing than the Romans had bargained for before their supplies had gone adrift. Attack after attack was beaten back and the Romans lost a thousand men before they drove the few defeated Dobunni farther into the hills and manacled the rest as captives. It was a stiff battle; and as Ostorius sited his new city of Corinium he may well have cursed the small untidy river and its inability to contain the water that ran off the hills and drenched the land so soggily. If he did, he was by no means the last to do so. But obeisances too were made.

Before science made us all so knowing, the source of any river offered a ready-made mystery; and anything to marvel at boundlessly affected people's lives. Religions, philosophies, and social orders are all guided in part by marvels, and rivers have borne their share of guidance in other than the practical ways of defence, transport, drainage, and so on. One must of course have preserved something of the quality of innocence to marvel nowadays at any natural phenomenon —everything having been sorted into its proper compartment of scientific explanation—but, given that, and some time to stare, there is much marvelling to be done.

My own staring at and around Thames Head was to some extent influenced by scientific knowledge: I know about rivers and their purpose, the organisation of the hydrosphere is clear to me, I know where the water comes from and goes to and why; I could easily have left it at that without writing down all these words—just as James Joyce might have left *Finnegans Wake* unwritten if he had not considered another river, the Liffey, as a suitable symbol of timelessness to frame it in. But earlier starers than I made much of what we think of as their ignorance, and their beliefs and some of the effects of those beliefs are worth recording.

All springs were meeting places and the mystery of the non-stop water bubbling from the ground must have been well discussed. No-one having thought of a spherical globe, the rational explanation was that the earth floated on the seas and that spring waters were, so to speak, leaks in the earth's surface. But not everyone was for rationalisation. Many preferred to think that there were river gods at work somewhere in the bowels of the earth—presumably operating pumping stations to keep the water on the go—and that these gods, like other gods, needed rewarding for favours dispensed. There is an immense mythology concerned with river-worship and the Thames has its fair quota—particularly at the source end.

At Lechlade, for example, twelve hundred years after the river had delayed the Romans in their battle for Thames Head, an annual sacrifice of three young virgins was being made to the Thames. One of the scribes of the monastic hospital there, St John's, has recorded that the prior was distressed at such paganism and publicly excommunicated the villagers pending more godly behaviour. But it was not as easy as that to allay superstition—particularly as, the following year, the river flooded over without apparent cause (it had been a relatively dry spring and summer) and the Lechlade crops were ruined. The primitive drainage was probably the cause, but to the Lechlade peasants it seemed that the river gods were demonstrating their anger for not having been paid their dues. Their spokesman was a man named Walker —a name that derived from his job, which was treading wool cloth in one of its manufacturing processes. (Walker worked at the looms in Corinium, which had now become Cirencester, the Romans and their battles and all their influences having been shrugged off.) Evidently he was shrewd, for he put it to the prior that though he and the other villagers were much concerned about being in the graceless state of excommunication, there was the matter of tithes to be paid to the priory as well as the economic life of the village to be carried on, and that neither could be done if the crops failed. This was patently true, and the prior compromised by allowing an annual sacrifice of three sheep instead of three maidens, pointing out at the same time that he was not sanctifying the practice of making obeisances to pagan gods but was acknowledging, on God's behalf, the villagers' simplicity. Both sides thus saved face. Not that it made much difference to subsequent events.

The following year three people, including an alderman of Cirencester, were drowned near Lechlade. This was taken to mean that the river god, having been denied his proper reward, was helping himself. The annual sacrifice of maidens was surreptitiously restored and was evidently continuing, with the principle slightly twisted, up to the seventeenth century, when 'Arabel Grey, the witch, was thrown from the weir for her wickedness'.

So far as I could establish, the name of the Thames god who had all these maidens and sheep and witches sacrificed to him to keep him sweet was Lud—though in time his name was dropped or forgotten and he became a nameless symbol or superstition. Lud was an Iberian or Celtic deity whose name was perpetuated by several ancient British kings—some of them probably as mythical as Lear and Cymbeline—and there was a temple for worshipping him in in the woodland glades that decorated the Thames Head eminence when the Romans fought for it. The temple was no more than a sacrificial stone altar in a clearing. Here the maidens were slaughtered and their bodies ceremoniously borne downstream to Lechlade, where they were committed to the water, which at this point was deep enough to cover them decently if they were weighted with holy stones. Not unnaturally, it is difficult to find any local people who know anything of river worship today—that is, who have conscious knowledge of it. But superstition, as always, lingers on. At the hairpin bend in the river a mile below St John's Lock I met a fisherman who, though he knew nothing about river gods, told me that the river hereabouts was known to be good for 'washing things away'.

'What things?' I asked him.

He hesitated for several minutes before replying. Then he said, 'I suppose you'd call it sin and that.'

'Sin?'

'Well, that's what you'd say if you'd done a murder, is it?'

'Guilt' was the word he was actually after, and I found the story in several Berkshire archives.

It seems that in the eighteenth century, in Buscot, which is a village a couple of miles downstream from Lechlade, there was a villager who was held in some awe because he was simple and simpletons were vaguely supposed to have been in

personal touch with God or the devil—according to the viewpoint held by the awed one. Like black cats, simpletons had a
foot in both camps. The manifestation of this simpleton's
simplicity was to demonstrate his disregard for companion-
ship and health by living in a hermitage of his own construction in the woods on the north side of the river (the village
is on the south side) and bathing daily at unpredictable hours
after a great deal of naked strutting up and down the river
bank. This behaviour was thought scandalous by some and
engaging by others; but it left no-one in any doubt as to his
simple-mindedness. He was left alone, and the kinder-minded
among the villagers occasionally put food on the river banks
for him. Presumably he supplemented these offerings by
catching fish or rabbits himself. He was known in the district
for over sixty years. Then, in 1776, he died, and his hermitage
was found to contain a confession of murder and an explanation that his hermitic withdrawal from the world had been
craftily organised with two objects : to escape earthly punishment by a pretence of dottiness that would allay suspicion,
and to escape heavenly punishment by rigorous daily dunking
in the Thames's 'waters of absolution'.

'It will be no great ordeal,' he wrote, 'to absolve me from
men's justice by leaving men to themselves, and from God's,
by the purifying waters of [the] river, which must slake
me of my crime.' Though I could find no-one but my fisherman who knew even the outline of the anecdote, there were
several conversational references to the Thames's 'purity' at
Buscot, and the tone and manner of the conversationalists
seemed to imply something rather more than chemical purity
—though they were vague when pressed for details. 'Oh, just
specially pure', was the most I could get in the way of defini-
tion. I did not press the matter—one reason being that I had
an appointment in Cirencester with my river transport and
its Captain (a statement that may raise some eyebrows but
which I shall explain).

Cirencester is not a Thames town (its river is the Churn), but it is the nearest town of any size to Thames Head, and after the fierce fighting that went on to establish it it seems churlish not to mention what has happened to it since its palmy Roman days, when it was the second largest town in Britain.

Rectangularly planned on the west bank of the Churn, with four main gates, it ranked as the capital of Britannia Prima, the gubernatorial prize among the four provinces into which Britain was divided, and lost its importance only when the Romans began to pick up their traps and leave in A.D. 400. Its structural beauty went when it was sacked and ruined by Saxon invaders in A.D. 577. The Saxons rebuilt (the site of the road junction being too important to abandon), but, like the Romans before them and everyone else since, found that rivers can be troublesome as well as helpful and that the Churn often overflowed and flooded the east side of the town; so their rebuilding was all westward onto drier ground.

The new Cirencester became a great centre of Christianity after King Alfred defeated the Danish invaders in A.D. 878. Guthrum, the Danish king, and all his court were converted and retired there into the new monastic college to meditate. The place became saturated with holy meditation and achieved such exalted status that King Canute held his great religious council there at Easter, 1020, having travelled up the Thames in the royal barge as far as Buscot, whence he completed the journey up into the Cotswolds overland with great pageantry, proclaiming new laws that were well received because they lightened Christianity with a little barbarism.

Soon after the Norman conquest a sizeable castle was built in the town by William Fitz Osbern, Earl of Hereford, a favourite of the Conqueror, and it might reasonably have been expected to stand for a thousand years. In the event it stood for fewer than a hundred. King Stephen destroyed it so completely during the battle royal with his wife Matilda over the succession to the crown that its site has never been definitely established. An abbey, built by Henry I in 1117, fared much better and lasted until the destruction of the monasteries by Henry VIII. Huge outbuildings adjoined the abbey, and here the abbot stored anything up to twenty thousand bales of wool —he, as Lord of the Manor, having the sole right to weigh it and control its sale and profits. Lively fairs were held to which merchants commuted from London, and the bales they bought were taken in torchlight procession to Lechlade, where they were loaded on to barges for transport to the capital. In the interest of public relations the barge horses were caparisoned in local wool cloth and the fleet was accompanied by hucksters who toured the Thames-side villages extolling the virtues of wool shrouds compared with linen—a virtue Charles II was later to endorse by enacting that 'henceforth all bodies shall be buried in woollens'.

From early in the thirteenth to the end of the eighteenth centuries Cirencester maintained a great commerce in wool, and the Thames was continually bearing laden wool-barges downstream to London. (Reading too was a wool town, and when we come to it I shall enlighten you about the rivalry between the two towns' bargees.) It also bore a great deal of more regal traffic—rivers offering by far the most dignified, if the slowest, arteries of transport until the modern scientific construction of roads began in the nineteenth century. Most of the monarchs barged it in their royal vehicles as far as Lechlade and then were entertained by the nobles or citizens of Cirencester as the town nearest the head of the river. One of them, Elizabeth I, fortunately arriving in the dry summer of 1592, commanded that she be borne in her litter the whole way along the river bank from Lechlade to 'the very first trickle of my fyne Thames' before going on to Cirencester, where her host, Sir John Danvers, presented her with 'a fayre cuppe of double gilt wirth xx£, given by the towne of Cysseter with an oration made in Latyn'.

George III came by road from Cheltenham, accompanied by his Queen (Charlotte) and three of their fifteen children, the party being received, some waffling scribe says, 'by a respectable party of Yeomanry, who served as guides to that noble mansion where they were received by the Venerable Earl of Bathurst and conducted to a most superb breakfast. After partaking of this most sumptuous repast his Majesty mounted his horse and the Queen and Princesses in open landaus took a view of those enchanting woods and groves which for more than fifty years have been the admiration of travellers of quality . . .' etcetera.

Cirencester lost its wool commerce with the re-centring of the trade in Yorkshire in the nineteenth century, and the railway put paid to its importance as a coach stop. Fireworks blazed over it in 1883, when its second railway station was opened. And after this display—which, the *Standard*'s correspondent said, had 'rarely been equalled and never exceeded in pyrotechnic magnificence'—it darkened and quietened into a little country town with a very big church. Tourists establish themselves there to tour the Cotswolds, and its biggest hotel, The King's Head, calls itself 'An Ancient Hostellerie'. It was there I joined my boat for the first part of the journey downstream.

3

A Link with the Severn

I

THIS vessel parked outside the hotel in the Market Place was an amphibious motor-car called an Amphicar. I know nothing of its mechanism, but in appearance it is like any small touring car, has a collapsible top, is built rather high off the ground with a flat under-belly, and, in addition to its four wheels, has twin screws projecting under the boot. A similar vehicle belongs to a friend of mine, John Worsley, who is an ex-naval officer—an artist by profession—and likes chugging about on road and river in this conveniently adaptable conveyance as a reviver between the ceremonies of the magic but exhausting business of art. Worsley's Amphicar was to bear me up and down the London end of the river, but it would have been quite impracticable for him to take time off for the complete exploration I had in mind, so I had made contact with another Amphicar owner living in Gloucestershire, Willie Hyne (as I shall call him here), and he had agreed to convey me as far as Oxford.

The Amphicar naturally must be driven down a slipway into the river, and we found an ideal gentle slope just above Lechlade, where the Coln runs into the Thames.

The counties cemented together here by river and road are Gloucestershire, Wiltshire, Oxfordshire, and Berkshire, and for a short stretch of the river below Lechlade one can throw a stone into each of them.

It used to be a favourite ploy of children to be taken to

some spot where they could straddle a boundary line and stand
with a foot in each of two counties, or jump from one to the
other shouting the counties' names as if some marvel were
involved. And perhaps one was. Too many quarrels in mankind's history have been concerned with the establishment of
the frontiers between 'ours' and 'theirs'—parochially no less
than internationally—and because rivers form natural lines
of demarcation the fact that, except in grave emergencies,
we no longer erect bastions of defence along their banks, or
otherwise warn strangers off, may be taken as a sign of a
change for the better in human behaviour. But although
frontiers and boundaries are a heritage of primitive tribal
strife they also designate the convenient division of juris-
dictive or administrative powers. The modern English term
for an administrative division, 'county', is the Norman equivalent—ex *cunté*—of the Saxon 'shire'—ex *scir*, meaning in
Old English 'division'—and thirty-nine of the fifty-three
English and Welsh counties have the suffix 'shire' in their
names. The ones that haven't—and of these Middlesex,
Surrey, Essex, and Kent are particularly my concern because
they flank the Thames—were once undivided Kingdoms;
but the shires were divisions of bigger Kingdoms like Mercia
and Wessex. Alfred, who was King of Wessex, had an 'ealdorman' responsible to him for each of his shires; but later kings
appointed 'shire-reeves' to the regional governments. The
holders of these appointments have become aldermen and
sheriffs and their authority, like their titles, has shrunk a
little; but they keep their titular dignity and importance in
local government.

The demarcationary importance of rivers has shrunk a
little too, and it is common to find towns that have grown from
settlements that once faced each other with bitter enmity
across the water being administered by a single authority;
but this is a matter of convenience, and rivers, like aldermen
and sheriffs, still pack a lot of theoretical legal power. For
example, the tidal part of any British navigable river, plus
the bed it flows on, belongs to the people (legal ownership

being vested in the Crown), and everyone has a right to put a craft on it and fish in it, though the right to use the banks or foreshore depends on prescription and custom. But above the point where the water ceases to be tidal (Teddington in the case of the Thames) rivers are the private property of the owners of the land they pass through, though in practice this means the bed of the river only, the flowing water itself being impossible to own unless taken away in a container. Private owners may not play Old Harry with rivers if their interference is going to alter the natural flow into neighbouring lands. If, for example, they want to divert a river to turn a mill or decorate a garden they must see to it that the diversion does not alter the character or quantity of the water after it leaves their boundaries.

But these 'musts' and 'must nots' remain very largely theoretical; and when men have found it convenient to alter the character of rivers—by polluting them, for instance—they have speedily superseded common law by Acts of Parliament which allow them to divert, diminish, and pollute as they please. Pollution of the Thames is a noxious subject several eminent potamologists have said some disconcerting things about, and I shall voice these abroad in my own way and time —the time being when we get to the heavily polluted stretches of the river. At Lechlade the water is relatively pure —and looks it—and as we chugged downstream at four knots I preferred to riffle through my broodings on the *Anglo-Saxon Chronicles* and other repositories of historical reportage and consider the part played by the Coln, the Leach, and the Thames in the division of the land hereabouts.

The Romans, who were orderly in matters of administration, used the Thames throughout its length to divide midland from Southern England; but in the Dark Ages that followed their departure—and Dark Ages are synonymous with dark pages of history, for there are no authentic records of the details of the Nordic invasions—there were so many invasions, repulsions, and annexations of territory that only a very confused picture of the lines of demarcation remain. It is certain,

however, that King Alfred abandoned the idea of a boundary
formed by the Thames above its esturial waters and divided
his kingdom from the Danish invaders' territory artificially.
This was partly because, as I have shown, the upper reaches
of the river were so marshy that its course was often undefin-
able; also, where its course was defined and the surrounding
area dry, it was too narrow and too shallow to form an
effective barrier to determined troops (undetermined troops,
and even civilians, wouldn't have had much trouble crossing
it either). But with the Norman conquest and the development of the feudal system it was necessary to define boundaries accurately, because Norman feudalism was wholly
territorial : a duke was overlord of a province, his barons held
strictly defined areas allotted by him (and in exchange they
were bound to give him forty days of military service every
year), the knights held smaller areas of land granted by the
barons, and the peasants smaller areas still. So everyone had
to have precise details of the extent of the land that could be
disposed of or that had to be tilled.

Though in theory either the Coln or the Leach could have
formed the eastern boundary of the Duke of Gloucester's
dominion, the practical difficulty of deciding the course of
either in such marshy terrain was great. A similar difficulty
precluded the choice of the north-to-south track that forded
the Thames at Lechlade, for it was bogged down except at
the droughtiest times. The Norman division of the two counties was eventually designated by a less watery boundary than
either the Thames's two headstreams or the track offered.
Great loads of timber, felled in the Oxfordshire forests, were
brought up the Thames and thrown into the marshes. This
piling up went on until the baulks formed first a causeway
and finally a palisade. The spaces in the palisade were then
filled with stone and the resultant wall stretched north as far
as Burford. To little effect, however. The enormous weight
proved too much for the soggy ground and the wall sank
almost visibly. By the year 1100 no trace of it was left. But a

D

century and a half later, when the land had dried out somewhat, the toppled stone blocks lay on the drained surface in a
long line and were salvaged and transported down the Thames
to Oxford, where they were used in the building of the earliest
of the colleges (probably Merton, though there is much
academic speculation about the claims of Balliol and University). So what had been designed as a division of suzerains
became an enclosure of learning.

It was much easier to separate the dominions of Wiltshire
and Berkshire because the north-south track that crossed the
Thames at Lechlade was clearly defined on the south side of
the river, the ground being firmer here, and a natural boundary line was thus evident. But natural and evident though it
was, it did not keep its boundary status for long. The sporadic
private wars of dukes and barons—often waged with monastic influence—shuttled the boundary to and fro across the
road with such speed that the border peasantry were often
doubtful about the lords they served. One such peasant,
tackled by a border baron returning from a clash in which
the Berkshire boundary had been pushed as far west as Cricklade, first made obeisances and then sprang to the attack,
using an iron goad with which he feebly went through the
motions of pricking out the armoured warrior's eyes.

'How is this, oxherd,' the baron said; 'dost thou serve me
or deny me?'

'My lord, or my lord's enemy, in whichever case you may
be, I know not. Here is my land, with my beasts upon it,
granted by my lord of Gloster as I suppose. But time and
again I am bidden this way and that with my beasts before
me and behind me while I know not whose land I serve and
must therefore bid my lord, if so you are, my faithful service,
and my lord's enemy, if that be your state, my utmost hate.
It is a time of too many changes for my fealty.' Unlike the
Vicar of Bray, in a later century and farther down the river,
this simple soul clearly had not the cunning to serve two
masters and phlegmatically accepted confusion as his lot.
His main concern was his job, which was to take the unyoked

oxen from the ploughman, settle them in pasture, and prevent
them from being looted by raiders. That done, he was beyond
shadow boxing with boundaries; this was a matter for 'them'.
A thousand years have not altered this shrug-shouldered
resignation, and it is still 'they' who darkly order our lives
away from the courses we want them to take. (The course of
the boundary presently observed by Wiltshire and Berkshire
is a tiny river, the Cole, which was no more than a stream in
Norman days, and which runs into the Thames opposite the
Coln.)

Reflecting on all this as we moved downstream in our four-
knot Amphicar, I found we had passed Kelmscott, which I
wanted to visit. We had also emerged from the river to avoid
the thick rushes that were gumming up the screws and were
making a detour round the roads skirting the meadows on
the south bank.

This was the western limit of Atrebate country in the tribal
days, and over the river was Dobunni country; and though
the two tribes were twain in their Celtic inheritance they
were never to show more enmity than in their last great battle
before the Romans came and thrust them back from both
banks of the river across which they had faced each other so
bitterly.

II

The immediate cause of this battle—if there was one—is not
known, but a spy's-eye description of it exists. The spy was a
Roman who was either anonymous or cryptic and signed
himself in his report merely 'C', which may have been numeri-
cal nomenclature like James Bond's or the initial of his name.
He was evidently a spy of some skill and daring, for he had
penetrated thus far west when his countrymen were still
battling for the Thames estuary. Evidently he had been in
England before (possibly as a trader) and knew how to avoid
suspicion. His purpose was to disclose diplomatic and military

weaknesses, and he was observant and shrewd in his deductions.

It was a bitter winter, and after the proper salutations to his superiors he describes the setting:

'The country here is cloaked in frost and ice which the people have learnt to cope with as it is an annual hazard, and we would do well to prepare ourselves similarly if we are not to suffer a disadvantage. The wheels of chariots are bound with strips of pelt and bound shoes are worn by horses and men. It is not country for battle, for the ground is tangled with undergrowth and small trees and in warmer times is marshy and insecure. But this the tribes ignore. They are so fierce in their enmity that they will take the greatest risks and bring to themselves the greatest obstacles to strategy if by doing so they can bring nearer the time to snatch at each other's throats.

'Obeying my orders I journeyed westward to this spot encountering many troubles which are of no relevance to my report. The distance is a hundred and fifty miles[1] as I judge and it has often seemed longer, such is the weather and the shape of the land and the uncouth living I have had to endure with these Britons. In my many parts I have been swineherd, physician, merchant, soothsayer—all to effect a disguise of friendship.

'This trifling river, Tamesis, of which the warring tribes make so much as a battle-line between them, seems of no consequence. Here in the west where I am (near its source, is my intelligence) it is nothing that could not be forded by our cavalry. But it can be treacherous because its banks are undefined and its seepage has extended the bogs for a great distance to north and south. Nothing could be grown here until it is engineered and dried out. Yet the tribes battle for it as if their lives depended on its muddy water.

1. The Roman mile was *mille passus*, a thousand paces, or 4,855·625 feet. Clearly he had been following the river, the twists and turns of which add considerably to the crow's-flight distance from London.

'Which brings me to the heart of my purpose.

'As I said, it is winter. The river itself is in depth here less than the height of a man, but it is frozen from the top nearly three cubits down, and the marshland all round is solidly frozen, with the reeds and rushes frozen together by the moisture on their surfaces so that they are boulders of ice strewn about on the frozen bog.

'The tribe of Atrebate recently determined to launch an attack north of the river against their enemy, the Dobunni. In this they were helped by the Catuvellauni, who also hold the north bank of Tamesis but farther to the east and also have a great hatred of the Dobunni, and, as I discovered when I put myself among them as a pedlar selling baubles (for which all Britons have a high regard), had crudely sent emissaries to the Atrebates to offer to reinforce the attack on the Dobunni flank if the salient across the river should prove successful.

'The attack was made two days ago, and I have delayed this only to be able to say who has won and who lost—a question I regret to say I have no true answer to. Indeed, to be truthful, I cannot say who was attacking and who defending, for these Britons have no refinement in these matters and are for ever certain to be at each other in twos and threes, if not in full battle. (If two should meet higher up the river where it is only a stream they will cross and do each other to death, so I have heard.)

'The baying of wolves was the first sign. Where the marshes end and the thick woods begin (which is where both tribes have their huts of timber and mud) the animals gathered, hearing the spilling of blood before it was spilt, like the soothsayers in the hills of Rome. That was three nights back. In the morning the frenzy of battle broke the day while the night fires were still smoking among the trees. Charioteers and infantry of the Atrebates came rushing across the marshes with a muffled thundering of bound feet on the ice. Their war cries froze the blood. They reached the river and a few chariots crossed to mow down the Dobunni with their knives

—or so was the intention. But the Dobunni too had heard the baying wolves and mounted their attack. The two forces clashed head to head with such confusion that is impossible to describe. Perhaps a thousand men went into battle, hand to hand and chariot to chariot. And then in the same day some Catuvellauni came from the east and joined the fight. But to little purpose. For all of them are like wild things, having no strategy or plan but to charge and kill. Prisoners are useless. No-one is left alive except he kills every attacker. Across and across the frozen river they battled while snow fell heavily. As the foremost ranks piled up their dead the remainder fought upon the corpses. Extermination could be the only end of such madness. And as the early winter night settled the snow fell too, covering the chaos of slaughtered men and beasts. The river of ice was coated with blood, and as I see it many weeks will pass in this cold country before the ice gives way and the blood is gone.

'We would do well to counter the terrible fierceness of these tribesmen with cunning, using only a small number of our soldiers to meet a large, and use ambushes, ground pits, and any kind of trap to defeat them, for their vows are against surrender, and if they would but use some design in their warring they would be greater than the Carthaginians.'

III

However grim the battles of men among themselves, their tussles with the elements can be longer, sometimes even grimmer. Earth, air, fire, and water are all accepted as death-dealing as well as life-giving. But water is characterised by unruly behaviour: it seeps and bubbles invisibly underground, spreads itself in floods, bears diseases, is often unpredictable and always potentially tremendous in its power. 'Ocean, thou mighty monster', someone sings in the opera *Oberon*; but the smaller waters of the Thames seem just as monstrous to anyone drowning in them. As for the extensive sogginess of the valley it runs in—this has posed a problem far from easy to solve.

Water can be drained from land vertically and laterally— downward through the subsoil or along the surface (or beneath it) through channels or pipes. The ploughed furrow is a natural drain that conducts surplus water to ditches surrounding a field, whence it may be further conducted directly into streams and rivers or be absorbed. But land cannot be ploughed if it is a quagmire, and if the lower soil is not absorbent enough the marsh that soddens it has to be dried out by other means.

The oldest and most obvious ways of dealing with the marshy land flanking a river are to widen the course of the river to include the marsh—in which case you get a bulbous section of the river but no reclaimed land; lower the river bed so that the capacity of the watercourse is greater and it will assimilate the drained water from the marsh; or dig ditches across the marsh and connect their ends to the river. That these methods have been used in many places along the Thames is evident. But who used them, and when, is less evident. The Romans, who were knowledgeable about canals and other waterworks (having gained much of their knowledge from the Dutch, than whom no-one knew more about inundations), probably directed many of them. But cartographers were rare until the fourteenth century, and the few earlier maps of the upper Thames area that exist are fanciful without being particularly useful to the seeker after evidence. County records and diaries are sometimes more revealing. One comes across such references as 'Seth Hogben died this Shrovetide digging the Great Ditch, the bank collapsing on him and others'; 'From Shifford we trapesed across fields inundated by bog and the spring sowing washed away'; 'I begit of my manne that the dam[ming] of the river wd my schef himme and so it is, he is gonne [and] the damme byrst and the river running over'. From Kelmscott all the way down to Oxford and beyond people have drained the marshes, and, later, lovers have lain in the lower meadows and heard

the subterranean waters. But like the tilling of fields and the
sowing of seed, the reclamation of land has gone on for a long
time; and it has been so much a part of everyday husbandry
that few people have thought it worth mentioning. The disasters one glimpses in such snatches of records as I have quoted
were minor ones, scarcely worth mentioning either, since they
ended in nothing more astonishing than death or a lost crop.
The imagination is not captured by the humdrum.

Everyone, however, is interested in something that can be
described—as such things often are—as A Grand Project.
Such an enterprise has to promise difficulty, danger, the ex-
denditure of big sums of money, and a result that will benefit
everybody. When it was envisaged in 1783 the Thames-
Severn Canal exactly filled the bill.

IV

The eighteenth century was the great age of canal building in
England. Swift and easy transport between industrial towns
and the ports was essential if the volume of exports was to be
maintained and the economy secured. Railways had not
arrived, and even the main trunk roads were in no condition
to take commercial traffic; nor were the road vehicles of the
time big enough to convey bulky goods in quantity. To link
the main rivers with artificial waterways was clearly the
answer. Private owners of coalfields and other centres of
industrial productivity, having an eye to the main chance,
readily supplied the capital for the construction of canals that
would speed their own exports, and Parliament enthusiastic-
ally dipped into the national cash-box to supplement private
investment.

To connect the two biggest rivers of England, the Thames
and Severn, and thereby form an inland link between London
and Bristol, was obviously a good idea. It was tossed around
and discussed, financed, planned, begun, and completed.
This took six years. (George III viewed the work in progress

during his visit to Cirencester on 19th July 1788 after that
sumptuous repast and view of the enchanting woods and
groves) and told the Earl of Bathurst that it was 'a demned
mighty piece of work'.

It was. Three thousand men were employed on its construction and it had necessitated piercing the Cotswolds with a
tunnel two-and-a-half miles long—the longest in England at
the time. This was no easy job. Tunnels were planned—and
still are for that matter—by sinking shafts at intervals to discover the nature of the subsoil; but this can be done only
when the surface land is reasonably level. Tunnelling beneath
hills sometimes meant an erratic course, since experimental
shafts could rarely be sunk and therefore no indication of the
nature of the obstacles in the form of impenetrable rock or
underground springs could be obtained. Thomas Winder, a
worthy of the village of Coates, where the southern entrance
to the tunnel was located, made gloomy prophesies about its
construction. 'I must remind your learned body', he wrote to
the President of the Royal Society, 'that rivers, like human
creatures, are disinclined to have their intimate structure
prodded and revealed and altered so that they are uncertain
of their destination and route. Like mankind too they are
separate and unalloyed and wed with each other by their own
designs and not for designs that are thrust upon them by
others without, if they are to prove useful in society. This
melding of our two great waterways is not to be wished by
them and we should leave it undone, otherwise disaster may
surely come upon us all for our stupid designs.'

Rather surprisingly, the President, Joseph Banks, seems to
have been to some extent impressed by Winder's eccentric
insight into the Thames's supposed resentment towards the
idea of being linked with the Severn, and promised an inquiry.
But his promise was probably intended to be no more than
soothing, for there is no record of any inquiry being held.

However dotty the theory behind Winder's prophesies of
disaster, troubles of varying magnitude certainly ensued.
There was great argument about the parliamentary grant to

be made for the work, and this was followed by temporary
adjournment of the project while MPs debated other more
urgent aspects of the industrial revolution. When work at
last began there were delays caused by the difficulty of re-
cruiting labour at a time when the coal and iron industries
were attracting workers to the midlands and north; by sub-
sidences which twice caused the canal to be re-routed; by
continual pumping operations when underground springs
broke into the tunnel; and by the prosecution of one of the
overseers for perjury (he had been a witness in a case of rape
and had falsely sworn to the alibi of the accused man—one
of his own workmen). All these major delays were irritated
and protracted by spells of bleak weather and a general
attitude of indolence that seemed to infect everyone from the
constructional engineers to the bargees who took away the
excavated earth. Whether Thomas Winder had been spreading alarm and despondency is impossible to prove; but no
doubt he was allowing himself a gleeful rubbing of hands as
he read of canals long completed that were already the life-
blood of the nation's commerce while the Thames-Severn
languished and often nearly died in what the Bristol author
of a pamphlet on 'The present State of Communication and
Correspondence in Our fair Land' called 'disgraceful in-
anition'.

At last, however, in 1789, just a few months after
George III had signified his royal interest by looking at the
work in progress, the canal was opened. The damming gates
were raised and the waters of the two rivers flooded the canal
and, in what another pamphleteer called 'sisterly affection',
mingled halfway at the junction with another canal, the
Stroudwater. The first barge, laden with gifts from the citizens
of London to the citizens of Bristol, was drawn along the
towpath 'by two strong horses fettled splendidly in ribbons
and brasses' to the Coates entrance to the tunnel. There the
motive power was taken over by 'leggers'—men who lay on
the decks of the barges and propelled them through the tunnel
by pushing their feet against notches cut into the tunnel walls.

At the other end, below the village of Sapperton, horses again took over and the gift barge was welcomed by 'a great crowd singing airs from Mr Dibdin and making gay with many flutes and suitable nautical noises'. On the return journey with reciprocal gifts the following day one of the leggers, Jonas Meldrum, somehow wrenched his foot in one of the wall notches and was disembarked at the Cirencester end of the canal and taken 'to be bandaged and cared for by the Earl of Bathurst's physician at the expense of his Lordship'. The barge was delayed overnight while Meldrum, a London man, was patched up and news of the delay was taken ahead to London by coach. The oral message became greatly distorted in transit and Meldrum's mishap was so exaggerated that he was given a hero's welcome at London Bridge and 'a purse of money from the Aldermen and Sheriffs for his trouble'.

Similar mishaps in the tunnel were not uncommon—though subsequently they went unexaggerated and unrewarded.

Smuggling and sabotage, on the other hand, were extremely profitable. Tea had become the national drink and tobacco the national habit, and since both carried exorbitant rates of import duty the professional smuggler had become as common as the bootlegger was to become in America's period of prohibition. The best people kept their personal smugglers in full employment, and the organisational centres for these professionals were the inns in ports and along river and canal routes. The Tunnel Inn was built at Coates for the men who legged the barges through the tunnel, and it was a most convenient headquarters for the Thames-Severn smuggling industry. Here information was passed, contraband routed and deliveries arranged. (Only a few years earlier, in 1777, the English diarist Parson Woodforde recorded: 'Andrews the smuggler brought me this night about 11 o'clock a bagg of Hyson Tea 6 pound weight. He frightened us a little by whistling under the parlour window just as we were going to

bed. I gave him some Geneva [gin] and paid him for the tea
at 10/6 per pound.'

All down the river there were collection points for small
packages of tea, tobacco, sugar, and rum, and these were
redistributed from nearby inns. Ten shillings and sixpence a
pound for duty-free tea meant that the smugglers were en-
joying a comfortable living, for seven and a half million
pounds of tea were being smuggled into the country annually.
Three million pounds a year distributed among the riders of
the contraband wagon meant that more and more people
tried to jump on it, and this in turn led to ugly incidents
caused by trying to keep them off. Gang fights were common
and these frequently led to the disposal of beaten-up bodies
in the canals and rivers. Thirteen were dredged up from the
Thames in one year—and this was after the Prime Minister,
Pitt, had reduced the import duty on tea and made smuggling
less profitable. As for sabotage, time and time again barges
were sunk by would-be bandwagon jumpers who got themselves in disguised form into the crews and skilfully drilled
holes in the barges' bottoms in nice time for 'rescue' by their
confederates on the banks. On one occasion, though, the
drilling was mistimed and a barge was sunk in the tunnel of
the canal. It took three days for a sufficiently powerful wind-
lass to be brought from Bristol and another three days for the
barge to be salvaged. All this time, of course, traffic was held
up; and when eventually the canal was cleared there was a
barge queue stretching down the Thames from Shifford to
Oxford—best part of a dozen miles. Bargees had come ashore
and set up camps where they discussed the situation. They
held meetings and tried to dream up means of getting com-
pensation for their losses, but there was no authority responsible and the meetings ended in vulgar abuse and smoke from
churchwarden pipes—most of the abuse coming from fishermen complaining about the disruption of angling.

By 1825 the smuggling of tea was no longer worth while,
because of the reduction of duty, and though there were
plenty of other goods that were worth evading tax on, the

heart of the contraband industry seemed to be weakening and the riverside inns were losing their importance as nerve centres. Canals were on the brink of losing their importance too. The railway was about to supersede them. Supersession was slow considering the speed at which railways were being laid and the even greater speed at which the trains ran on them (the three-day Bristol–London barge journey was reduced to two hours); but it was relentless. Some canal companies appeased their shareholders by selling out to the railway companies at inflated prices during the boom years of railway development in the middle of the century; others thought such a course treacherous and belligerently said they'd see the railways damned before they gave in. But they were defending a crumbling citadel. The canals were doomed. All the government intervention—manifested in the form of Railway and Canal Traffic Acts intended to equalise the canals' chances in a steam-sped world—failed to do more than delay by a few years the dereliction on many of the smaller canals.

The Thames-Severn lingered on until 1911. A small faction of enthusiasts was as reluctant to see its end as Thomas Winder had been to see its beginning; led by a chartered accountant called Murfin they called public meetings, wrote to Members of Parliament, and handed out leaflets at street corners. But their pleas fell on stony ears and stonier pockets. Mr Murfin and his chums could do no more than stand with bared heads as the last barge officially to use the canal passed into the Thames on Easter Day 1911. 'There is no chance', he wrote to the *Morning Post*, 'that the Thames–Severn canal will ever be forgotten.' But if it hasn't been forgotten it has achieved a state of gloomy desuetude. The towing paths have vanished in the overgrowth, parts of the tunnel roof have fallen in, and the entrances are choked with weeds.

4

A Ghostly Encounter

I

FROM the southern entrance to the tunnel at Coates we
drove back to Thames Head. Willie Hyne's remark that we
seemed to be back to square one was mildly admonitory, but
it didn't alert me to his potentialities as a counsellor on literary
matters—even when he added, 'If I were you I'd let's hop it
to Oxford—plenty there to write about—you know it's the
city of dreaming spires?'

'Kelmscott first,' I told him. 'There's a headless boatman
there I wanted to make the acquaintance of.'

Knowledge of this body had come my way in a place very
remote from the Thames and at a time that now also seemed
remote. At Dar-es-Salaam, where I had an overnight stop in
1959 before catching a plane to bring me back to London,
I had dinner with a man who was born in Eaton Hastings, a
tiny village half a mile downstream and across the river from
Kelmscott. He'd been in the Colonial service all his working
life and in thirty years had never been back to England. 'I
usually go down to Jo'burg or up to Cairo when my leave
comes round; maybe as far as Paris. But not U.K. Too
strong a grip. Ghosts, you know. Nostalgia. Whatever you
like to call it. I'd never get back here. I've done with
it now. I'll retire somewhere else—Australia, probably.
What they're doing in U.K.—I'd probably find my little
village full of bloody great skyscrapers.'

He didn't disclose his name, and I didn't ask him. Nor did

I record his dialogue. But I put him down in my notebook in some outlining phrases (I called him 'a Carstairs or Carruthers with an ant-proof trunk full of *Blackwood's*'), and I haven't saddled him with anything out of character in the way of phrases. He waxed loquacious in the manner of a club-fender raconteur, and the story he told me stuck in my mind as firmly as the sound of his voice designating his drink as 'pinkers'.

'There was always this tradition. Ghosts clank about in hundreds of English villages. If they aren't there people make 'em up. There was one at Kelmscott, the next place up the river from Eaton Hastings, but on the other bank. But I don't know if he was made up. My grandfather on my mother's side used to tell me he'd seen him when he was a boy. When were the times they used to chop people's heads off for sheep-stealing? Fifteen hundreds, sixteen hundreds? Kelmscott Manor's Elizabethan, I know that. Anyway, whenever it was, there was this man who lived in Kelmscott village who used to be a boatman on the Thames. I don't know what his name was. He never had a name that I heard. He was just called "the boatman". I suppose he was part of a transport service up and down the river to Oxford. They used to load stone at Radcot Bridge, which is down towards Oxford from Eaton about a mile, and I suppose he helped load it or it was his boat or something.

'Anyway, it was at Radcot he was caught sheep-stealing; or supposed to have been sheep-stealing, but he denied it. The trouble is, they don't go into the details in these old stories. Are you caught with a bloody great baa-ing animal tucked under your coat, or what? The point of the tale was that he was never brought up in front of the beak; the farmer whose sheep it was he was supposed to have pinched took the law into his own hands. Chopped his head off with a butcher's cleaver there and then. Well, I say "there and then"; it may have been later; but whenever it was it was at Radcot Bridge. And the tale went that the boatman had to walk all the way back to Kelmscott without his head, looking for justice or the

peace of his own bed or something. So the towing path was
haunted by him—that was the tale. There wasn't much
detail about when you might see him—I remember I was
always trying to get my grandfather to tell me that, but he
didn't know or wouldn't tell. But I and my chum who lived in
Kelmscott used to try like mad to see this ghost. Honestly,
we did everything—stayed out till dusk, stayed out all night
once, watching. But no sign. I don't think we ever doubted
the ghost existed. Anyway you heard about him all the time—
he was a legend all round, you see, parents used to threaten
their disobedient kids with him—"I'll bring the boatman to
you", they used to say. And naturally we wanted to see him,
my chum and I. A man without a head—you can imagine
how we wondered if there was just a hole in the neck where
the head was and if you could see down it into the stomach,
like looking down a well. It was *in*teresting, a matter of *in*-
terest, you see—not child sadism like pulling wings off flies,
but curiosity, we wanted to see this thing for ourselves. I hope
you get me?'

I said I understood him very well, that his grandfather on
his mother's side was vague about details but that he and his
chum from Kelmscott tried everything they knew, honestly.
I also offered him another pinkers, which he accepted.

'Then came the evening we both went fishing down to
Radcot Bridge. The trout there were easy and we stayed there
quite late, it being summer and dusk not till almost nine. I
don't think we'd been thinking specially about the boatman—
I hadn't anyway—and we certainly hadn't mentioned him
aloud——'

'Ah,' I said, anticipating the payoff the way one does when
people are boring you and you've passed the limit of snake-
like fascination. 'At last—suddenly—he emerged out of the
dusk.'

'Eh? Oh no. We never saw him that night or any time. It
was a different thing altogether that turned me up. The
bridge, Radcot Bridge, is just a stone one with three arches,
supposed to be very old. It carries the Faringdon road over

the river and there are trees and thick shrubs on both sides
of it, on both river banks. We always parted here, my chum
and I, because his village is on the north side of the river and
mine on the south and there's nowhere nearer you can cross.
So we always walked home on opposite banks shouting to
each other till we came to my village and he went on to his.
So we did this night—or started to. Then I got my foot
caught in this rabbit hole—whatever it was. I couldn't get
it out—wedged, you see?—and I got a bit scared, imagining
being fixed to the spot for ever. My chum called out what was
up? And I shouted back to him I'd got stuck. He jeered at
first, knowing I was scared, letting me sweat on the scare—
just as I'd have done if it had been him with his foot stuck. It's
funny how when anything like that happens you suddenly
realise how dark and cold the night is. A minute before it had
just been ordinary dusk on a warm summer evening, but the
scare turned it dark and cold at once. I heard him go off
jeering; and although I knew he was only scaring me a bit
more and that he'd come over and help release me in a
minute, or I'd release myself by digging round my foot or
something, I knew I was going to shout out for help if I was
scared much longer; and that would have been humiliating.

'I got a grip on myself for a second and wrenched my foot
round—the pain killing the scare, you see?—until something
gave way. Not my foot—though I thought for a minute I'd
torn it off—but the earth it had got jammed in. My foot
was out and I hopped around on the other one, not shouting
now but doing the heroic stuff—you know how kids do?—
concealing my agony behind clenched teeth. My chum started
on his way back, a bit bothered because I'd stopped shouting,
I suppose, and I could see him across the river in the dusk.
I collapsed onto the ground in a dramatic way and stayed as
still as I could, still making the clenched-teeth hero effect.
Then I saw that the rabbit's hole I'd twisted my foot away
from wasn't really a rabbit's hole at all but a sort of cavity
dug out under the ground, and that what I'd got my foot in
was only a crack in what you might call the ceiling of the

E

cavity. I'd exposed the cavity by wrenching my foot out and widening the crack. You see?'

I said I saw and tried to look expectantly agog for news of the cavity's contents. I was thinking in terms of a hoard of sovereigns. But the discovery was rather more grisly than that : a skull, cleft by what well may have been a butcher's cleaver.

That was my raconteur's story; and it was, so to speak, the other half of it that I was morbidly concerned with. What had happened to the body the head had been chopped from? After recovering from some queasiness the two boys had borne the skull to Eaton Hastings, anxious for self-centred sensation. The village bobby had taken charge and the skull had eventually been lost track of so far as my raconteur was concerned. But as he said, it at least proved that there must have been a body somewhere at some time, without its head, and that there was therefore some backing for the legend of the headless boatman. I was anxious to know if the legend still flourished and if anyone had seen the ghost lately. Ghosts—if they were Thames ghosts—were as interesting to me as everything else in my limning of the river.

II

A churchyard may in theory be a promising place for the giving up of ghosts, but the one at Kelmscott yielded none. It was too small to harbour much more than William Morris's grave; and the village (population one hundred and forty) was having its afternoon sleep when we arrived there. Not the slightest breath of curiosity about our presence as strangers could be felt. Even two schoolboys at the age of scientific curiosity didn't give the Amphicar a second glance. There was no malevolence about this lack of concern, nothing thwarting about the few faces that observed our arrival : Kelmscott was simply selfconsciously sleepy, determinedly playing the part of 'the typical English village'—a part made much of in the glossy postcard industry.

For once in my life I was stumped as to my approach. 'Has anybody seen a headless boatman lately?' is a ludicrous thing to ask anyway, but in a receptive atmosphere it could be answered in key. Here, I thought, I should only get a non-committal answer to a zany question, which is always disconcerting. And if I wrapped the question up in formal phraseology ('Excuse me, sir, but many years ago I heard the tale of a somewhat grisly manifestation of a poor decapitated wretch . . .') I should also get a non-committal answer, which would be even more disconcerting. I decided to leave the question unposed in any form for the moment and go and see Kelmscott Manor instead. Leaving Willie Hyne and his Amphicar to park themselves near the post office, I completed my tour of the hundred yards or so of village street and made for the big house.

William Morris bought the Manor in 1871, but it was three hundred years old then, described in the bill of sale as 'a gracious manor house of Elizabethan origin built of the local stone and with some three acres of meadow dividing it from the river'. Morris was a Thames man. He was born in Walthamstow, on the fringe of the river's northern marshes, and died in his Thames home in Hammersmith. Except during his travels in France and Iceland he was never far away from the river. He borrowed the name of Kelmscott for both his home in Upper Mall, Hammersmith, and for the Press with which he made his splendid contributions to typography and bookbinding; and he often brought the river into his prose and poetry—for example, in the description of Kelmscott in *News From Nowhere* and in *For the Bed at Kelmscott*, which I quote:

> The wind's on the wold
> And the night is a-cold,
> And Thames runs chill
> 'Twixt mead and hill,

But kind and dear
Is the old house here,
And my heart is warm
Midst winter's harm.
Rest, then and rest,
And think of the best
'Twixt summer and spring
When all birds sing
In the town of the tree,
And ye lie in me
And scarce dare move
Lest earth and its love
Should fade away
Ere the full of the day.
I am old and have seen
Many things that have been,
Both grief and peace,
And wane and increase.
No tale I tell
Of ill or well,
But this I say,
Night treadeth on day,
And for worst and best
Right good is rest.

In spite of an explosive temper, Morris was at heart a
gentle man with idealistic notions about living, art, and
letters. His daughter Mary, who inherited Kelmscott Manor
after his death in 1896, remembered this when she herself
made her will. She bequeathed the house to Oxford University when she died in 1938, together with an endowment of
£3000 and a stipulation that the house should be offered as
a home for the *emeriti* of Exeter (Morris's college), the Slade
School of Arts, the Ashmolean Museum, or the Bodleian
Library. Morris founded the Society for the Protection of
Ancient Buildings in 1877 and there was no doubt in my mind
that Kelmscott Manor would be an exemplar of his devotion

to the fine things of the past and his concern for the peaceful
retirement of literary men. I had thought of writing to the
Warden to ask for permission to see over the house and grounds
so that I might enjoy its graciousness and at the same time
ask any of the staff I took to be local whether they knew anything of the ghost of the headless boatman, but on second
thoughts I'd decided to make it a less formal visit and take
my chance on being conducted round the place.

You can, as they say, imagine my indignant surprise when
I found the grounds as choked with weeds as the Thames-
Severn tunnel and the house abandoned. I entered through
an open side door and walked through the empty rooms uncertain for a moment whether I was in the right house or even in
the right village; but of course I was. I thought of the Thames
running chill and the old house no longer kind and dear. What
had intervened to prevent the implementation of Mary Morris's
tribute to her father? I was to discover later that it had never
been possible to administer the bequest because of the in-
adequacy of the endowment and the lack of available funds
in the kitties of either Exeter College or the William Morris
Society. The house had been let to a succession of private
tenants and eventually the will clause had been declared in-
valid on the arguable legal ground that the bequest had never
been intended as a charitable trust. That decision having been
made in the High Court, the house reverted to the residuary
legatee of Miss Morris's property—the Society of Antiquaries, of which Morris had been an inactive member. But
this body had no funds to support the house and rack and
ruin had set in.

Fortunately, in the same week that I was indignantly uncovering this seemingly hopeless news there came a shot in the
arm for the Antiquaries in the form of a huge gift of money,
of which they quickly allocated £20,000 for the restoration
of Kelmscott. But I knew nothing of this as I went from room
to room moodily baffled by the emptiness and silence. I

thought of Morris and his immensely varied talents. His poems were perhaps too full of Thous and Werts and 'Twixts to be acceptable to modern ears; but his prose is firm and stern, the 'Hammersmith' carpets he turned out in the stables of the Upper Mall house and the furniture, fabrics, stained glass, wallpapers and other decorations he designed are collectors' pieces today. His idealistic socialism, manifested in his formation, in 1884, of the Socialist League, was one of the cornerstones of the modern socialist movement. And he was a lifelong rebel against the crude values of Victorian industrialism. And as I took in the abounding neglect I could think of no bitterer irony than that he was the principal founder of the Society for the Protection of Ancient Buildings.

I left the house by the same broken door and crossed the meadow to the river. There were thick growths of rushes along the banks, and in the mud above water level some loaches were churning about. (I couldn't remember where I'd read it, but it was firmly fixed in my mind that this fish has the unique power of turning its stomach into a spare lung and that it can therefore live out of water for longer than any other fish. It appeared that this might be true, because the loaches were high and dry and were showing no signs of breathing their last.) By an association of ideas I thought of the turmoil that must have gone on in Morris's mind when he was trying to decide where next to direct his creative powers. Since his manual activities extended from the weaving of cloth to the illuminating of manuscripts, and his literary ones from the invention of Norse sagas (as in *The Story of Sigurd the Volsung*) to the anticipation of fascism (as in *News From Nowhere*), he must continually have been faced with a choice of directions; even harder, having subdued the turmoil and made the choice, he must have been able to summon immense powers of concentration to keep him pegging away along a particular path when so many other paths radiated from his capacious intellect. One-man-bands of such varied harmonies are rare; they are symphonists who reverberate in the meditations of anyone who troubles to unplug his ears.

Morris's sinfonias of activity were booming through my own meditations as I strolled along the towpath towards its junction with the road back to the village. I am trying to establish (perhaps heavy-handedly—I am no Walter de la Mare) that I was, so to speak, poised with a foot on each of two planes, the meditative and the real; but unlike kids straddling two counties I wasn't delighting in the simple pleasure of my athleticism. I wasn't even aware of it. If it seems pretentious to say that I was meditating while walking back to the village on the seeming death of Kelmscott Manor contrasted with the creative abilities of its late proprietor, I'm quite willing to offer an alternative text: I was just mooning along the towpath. Whichever you accept you should understand that I was in one of those states of mind often called 'receptive' and associated, by those who have supernatural axes to grind, with 'Vibrations'.

I wasn't of course any more conscious of vibrations than of being poised on two planes; but I was very conscious indeed as I reached the junction of encountering a presence. Invisible of course, but not inaudible. There was, first, the very distinct sound of the swish of long grass. It was so distinct that I stopped and looked down and round to see if I myself was walking through verdure of some kind; but the path was continuously stony and bordered with nothing but dirt and a few close-bitten weeds. Besides, the swishing continued as I stood motionless. It was accompanied by the subdued sound that feet would make if they were stepping through long grass. There was another sound too—not unpleasant in itself but dreadful because of the association it conjured up in my mind: it was a slow bubbling noise, and I thought of it as the sound of blood being forced up through a severed jugular vein by a dying heart. These sounds seemed to be in turn approaching me, beside me, and retreating behind me. If I wasn't actually being passed by the ghost of the headless boatman I had at least been pretty successful with my self-persuasion.

As you see, I haven't made a production of this tale. If I were presenting it as fiction I should expect to have it bounced as being seriously flaired—its most defective bit of mechanism being the pre-conditioning I gave myself by looking up my notebook entry on the Dar-es-Salaam encounter and deliberately setting out to find anyone who'd had sight or sound of the ghost. I had also remembered very vividly my raconteur's childlike concern about whether you could look down the headless boatman's neck into his stomach, and it's quite easy to see that this might automatically have suggested to my mind the gruesome image of the bubbling jugular. Also, I had been wandering through an empty house, which may have aided my receptiveness to hauntings of one kind or another. I may in fact have convinced myself of the reality of the whole encounter simply because I wanted to. Whatever the causes and effects, my physical response was to feel sweatily cold. I turned up the road to the village keeping as near to an appearance of unhurried rumination as I could; but the distance wasn't enough to give me time to regain much composure. I found Willie Hyne trying to judge from his Thames chart if he could drive his Amphicar into the river nearabouts; but the charts revealed nothing of the angle of the river banks and whether or not they would make a slipway, and in any case, I told him, I'd as soon go by the road as far as Radcot Bridge and then enter the river there if there was a slip.

'What about this boatman, then?' he asked me.

I told him I'd dealt with the boatman and he was incurious enough not to want to take that matter any further.

'If you're going the road way, then, you ought to have a look at Friar's Court above Radcot. Funny old place it is— it used to be a what-d'you-call-it, a monastery.'

'Oh,' I said, looking, I hope, suitably surprised.

'Plenty to write about there, I sh'd think.'

There is in fact plenty to say in a general sense about the church's foundations along the Thames, and I shall say some of it in due course; but there's nothing special about Friar's

Court, and in any case, as we drove towards Radcot, made a northward detour through two villages called Clanfield and Bampton, and entered the river again a few miles farther down near Shifford Lock, I was more concerned with a time when Christianity was only weakly established in Britain. Alfred, that great Christian king, is supposed to have held one of his early parliaments at Shifford; but it was a pagan king, Penda of Mercia, who used the middle reaches of the Thames with permanent effect on England's history.

III

The seventh-century midland kingdom of Mercia stretched southward from the Trent and its king, Penda, became the most powerful ruler in Britain. He was fifty years old when he acceded in 626 and he lived another twenty-nine years before being slain in battle near Leeds. During that time he vanquished many of the Saxon states, and one of his greatest battles was against the kingdom of Wessex, which until his overlordship stretched from the south coast up to the Avon in the middle of England. Penda was determined to conquer the agriculturally important Chiltern Hills, which offered drained pasture and splendid arable land well elevated above the still undrained marshes that bordered the Thames through most of its middle reaches. In a series of battles that occupied him for the first twenty years of his reign he gradually forced the chieftains—they could scarcely be called kings —of the smaller states to endure his rule. His strategy was crafty and he was personally brave and strong (for anyone to live to the age of seventy-nine in Anglo-Saxon England was a testimony to toughness). By 640 he had extended his kingdom southward as far as the Thames and had made sporadic forays into what are now Surrey and Berkshire, crossing the river at Staines. He fought westward as far as the Saxon settlement at what was soon to become Reading. There he was forced back across the river, but within three months he had established his rule all along the north bank as far as Wallingford, where he once again forced a bridgehead south into Berkshire. But when he tried to extend his conquest westward along the line of the Thames he was defeated—as many had been before him and many more would be in the future—by the sogginess of the terrain. Men and beasts floundered in the bogs and were unpleasantly asphyxiated. The marshy land stretched for miles, and to cross the river except at the few fords needed engineering equipment that could only be hinted at in the travesties of pontoons and causeways that were constructionally possible. 'Penda's losses', the *Anglo-Saxon Chronicle* says, 'were more than he could perceive. He was served by faithful thegns[1] but they could not succeed in any affray when the ground subsided beneath them and they could only give their lives to fight back the engulfing marsh. He was forced to withdraw his men from the lower territory and settle them upon the upper where the land was dry. But so fierce and feared was he that the threat of his bands upon the upper bank was enough to maintain peace below. And attended by his etheling[2] and thegns he parleyed with Ine of Wessex and they agreed that henceforth the river should divide their kingdoms, Mercia from Wessex, and that their kinsmen of all generations to come should keep it so.' Which they did, so long as the kingdoms lasted—which wasn't long, for the Danish invasions were soon to cause the dissolution of territorial rule and the establishment of a king of the whole of England.

Between those events, though, the ethics of Anglo-Saxon fealty were demonstrably at their most noble. The *Anglo-Saxon Chronicle* is thick with tales of nobility—some of them demonstrating also that in any age women are likely to lead you into trouble. As for instance in one entry for the year 755.

'This year Cynewulf and the West Saxon witan deprived his kinsman Sigebert of his kingdom, except Hampshire, for

1. A thegn (or thane) was a freeholder of land granted by the king in exchange for military service.
2. Prince or heir apparent.

his unjust doings. And Hampshire he held, until he slew the ealdorman who longest abode by him. And then Cynewulf drove him up into the river country of Berkshire and he abode there until a swineherd stabed him at Privets flood, and he avenged the ealdorman. And King Cynewulf fought very many battles against the Mercians, sometimes gaining ground north of the river and sometimes falling back so that his kingdom in part was lost to him and gained to the Mercians, but they could use it not in much places for the bad land of the marshes.

'And so the battles endured for one and thirty years; and at the end of that time the river was still a trouble and not a joy as lesser rivers are; also are greater rivers a joy sometimes. And after one and thirty years he purposed to expel an etheling, who was named Cyneard: and Cyneard was Sigebert's brother. And the etheling learned that the King, with a small band, was gone to Merton [in Surrey, five miles south of the river and on one of its tributaries, the Wandle] to visit a woman; and he there beset him and surrounded the chamber on every side, before the men who were with the King discovered him. And, when the King perceived this he went to the door and there manfully defended himself, until he beheld the etheling, and then he rushed out upon him and sorely wounded him; and they all continued fighting against the King until they had slain him. And, upon this, the King's thegns, having discovered the affray by the woman's cries, each, as he was ready, and with the utmost speed ran to the spot. And the etheling offered money and life to each of them, and not one of them would accept it; but they continued fighting until they all fell, except one, a British hostage, and he was sorely wounded.

'Then, upon the morrow, the King's thegns whom he had left behind him, heard that the King was slain. Then rode they thither. And, at the town wherein the King lay slain, they found the etheling and those within had closed the gates against them: but they went then forward. And the etheling offered them their own choice of land and money if they would grant him the kingdom, and showed them that their kinsmen were with him, men who would not desert him. And they then said that no kinsman was dearer to them than their lord, and that they never would follow his murderer. And they, in turn, bade their kinsmen that they should go away from the etheling in safety. But the kinsmen said that the same had been bidden to those who before had been with the King, and that they themselves would now pay no more attention to such offers.'

All this chivalrous conduct involved far more than simple in-fighting round castle walls and locked chambers. The English weather was changeable enough to make the choice of a battlefield unpredictable. In twelve hundred years the climate has become a little more stable, and the terrain a great deal less shifty, but in the eighth century the heavy storms, plus the undrained meadows that were typical of all the low-lying country that in general characterised the south, combined to make big battles difficult. Extensive military organisation had vanished with the Romans. Fighting was mainly between small bands who fought on until one side was vanquished, and large areas were claimed by this simple king-of-the-castle technique. So Penda's conquests in Wessex were probably conquests less in the sense of actual occupation than in the sense of control by personality. And when he argued with the rival King of Wessex about the division of their kingdoms by the Thames he probably pointed out the common-sense aspect of making a boundary of the river. The valley land was for the most part unusable either for battle or agricultural production and had better be left alone. He had annexed the Chiltern Hills and Ine had kept the good wealds of Kent and Sussex. They were not unreasonable in assuming that their pact of separation would hold good for a thousand years.

In a sense it has. No rival states face each other across the river, but its course marks a change of character. Subtle differences of personality are noticeable in north-of-Thames and south-of-Thames people when cities straddle the river, as do Oxford and London. (Which inhabitants of Oxford, I wonder, were those referred to by Gerard Manley Hopkins in a letter of 1880 as 'stiff, stand-off and depressed'?) The difference emphasises the division of the city into two parts. And the differences are not only of dialect—though, as Professor Higgins would point out, the accents of Euston and Southwark are as of worlds wide apart. I do not propose to go into those differences of personality because I am myself involved—a southerner born in Surrey, within chucking distance of that Thames tributary the Wandle, where King Cynewulf misled himself into all that trouble through his lady —and I probably wouldn't be trusted as an objective critic. But you can take my word for it that Penda's judgement remains effective. The Thames, temperamentally as well as geographically, divides England.

IV

We—and now I mean Willie Hyne and me—were in the dividing river itself, approaching Oxford through a stretch of country that offered singularly few diversions, so I could reflect with detachment and equal benevolence on both Oxfordshire and Berkshire people and terrain. Thomas Fuller in his *Worthies of England* says of Berkshire that 'It may be fancied in a form like a lute lying along, whose belly is towards the west, whilst the narrow neck or long handle is extended towards the east. . . . It partaketh as plentiful as any county in England of the common commodities, grass, grain, fish, fowl, wool, and wood.' And although he does not suggest any fanciful shape for Oxfordshire he says 'It aboundeth with all things necessary for man's life and I understand that hunters and falconers are nowhere better pleased. Nor needeth there more pregnant proof of plenty in this place, than that lately Oxford was for some years together a court, a garrison and an university; during which time it was well furnished with provisions on reasonable rates.'

Fuller was writing in the seventeenth century, and the

court he was referring to was that of the first King Charles, who had made Oxford the centre of his operations during the Civil War. But this was by no means the first time a monarch had been associated with the city of learning (and, as Willie Hyne had hastened to remind me, of dreaming spires). King Alfred, a Berkshire man born at Wantage in or about 849, was both the first king of all England and the first educated English monarch. He visited Rome in his early years and set very great store by learning. He was an educator in the sense of being a writer and translator, and although the tale that he founded the university of Oxford isn't true, it is probable that he had the glimmerings of the idea of establishing an educational centre there in 879, soon after he had signed the treaty of Wedmore, which assigned the country north and east of a boundary stretching from Chester to London to the invading Danes and the rest to the Saxons—of whom he was of course king.

Alfred's capital was Winchester (mythically the Camelot of King Arthur), but he made a number of journeys to Oxford to meet the scholars from Europe he invited to discuss with him the dissemination of knowledge. One of these journeys was made in the simplest style and to combine two practical purposes: the meeting with the scholars and the trial of a new kind of ship which had been constructed to his own design by shipwrights at Reading. This was the design on which he based that of the longer, steadier, and faster warships that were eventually to defeat the Danes in their continual coastal invasions. Accompanied by his thegns and bishops Alfred came up from Winchester to Reading and there embarked in the new vessel, leaving everyone except a handful of personal attendants encamped on the high ground between the Thames and the Kennet (a mile or so to the east of my house) where, in 1121, Henry I was to lay the foundations of Reading Abbey. Alfred travelled in the most austere fashion, spending the time in meditation, the translation of Latin manuscripts, and the observation of the behaviour of the ship.

The journey to Oxford took ten days because there were of course no locks and the ship had to be manhandled up ramps every time a change in water level was encountered. At every such spot men had to be summoned from the surrounding countryside, and since the location of the weirs was often inconveniently at variance with the location of riverside settlements or villages there was bound to be delay. Also, there was a break in the journey at Wallingford, where the king disembarked and visited his birthplace, Wantage, where 'he was welcomed by all the people of that place and obeisances were made by the bishops who had come many miles to show their service and love and to minister to his health, which was not sturdy. He stayed in that place one night and then would not stop more but took his leave with blessings.'

Eventually he arrived at what is now Nuneham Park, three miles east of Oxford, and there disembarked and was ferried across flooded meadows in a small boat, taking with him his manuscripts. At the castle fortifications, which had been built up as part of the defences against the Danes, he met the foreign scholars and remained in conference with them for three days, discussing Saint Augustine, Boethius, Bede, and Orosius—whose works he translated—and seeking their advice on his proposals to educate the English, or at least to give them a foundation library. One of the many legends that have attached themselves to Alfred is that the tranquillity of Oxford's meadows and its convenient situation on a ridge of dry ground at a road and river junction (the Cherwell joins the Thames to the east of the city) inspired in him the vision of countless scholars converging on the city from all directions, there to be themselves inspired in the pursuit of knowledge.

Whether or not he had the vision—and it seems about as likely as that he burnt the cakes, since the meadows in those days were soggy marsh—the city certainly became a centre of scholarship; and it remained a tranquil hub in a wheel of midland industrialisation until the 1920s, when that later William Morris, Viscount Nuffield, re-invented the cheap motor-car (first turned off the conveyor belts of Detroit by Henry Ford) and set up his machinery at Cowley, south-east of the city. Thereafter tranquillity was confined to the college lawns, Christ Church Meadow, and the Botanic Gardens. The city was again to become a garrison (this time for American soldiers) in the second world war, and when the war was over and the soldiers had gone, architectural loyalists like Mr John Betjeman and practical planners like Mr Thomas Sharp (who was the corporation's consultant on planning matters) exchanged some cogent remarks in the press about the future of the city.

(The shape of the city, by the way—indeed its very existence—is determined by the course of the Thames, which, with the Cherwell, forms a U running moat-wise round the ridge on which the city is built. The river therefore offers a natural defence on three sides.)

Anyone could compile a hefty anthology of approving comments about Oxford and its natural and architectural beauties, and at least half of them would make reference to the Thames. Even in its less obvious manifestations the river has made its mark. 'The scent of the meadows' mosture', wrote Max Beerbohm in *Zuleika Dobson*, 'is the scent of Oxford. Even in the hottest noon one feels that the sun has not dried *them*. Always there is moisture drifting across them, drifting into the Colleges. . . . Yes, certainly, it is this mild, miasmal air, not less than the grey beauty and gravity of the buildings, that has helped Oxford to produce, and foster eternally, her peculiar race of artist-scholars, scholar-artists. . . . There is nothing in England to be matched with what lurks in the vapours of these meadows. . . .'

The meadow moisture is dealt with by Hilaire Belloc too, in a couple of carefully bad lines in his *Moral Alphabet*, where O stands for Oxford :

> The marshes in the neighbourhood can vie.
> With Cambridge, but the town itself is dry.

Cuthbert Bede in his Adventures of Mr Verdant Green stands in the meadow at the junction of the two rivers and says lyrically: 'The beautiful meadows lay green and bright in the sun; the arching trees threw a softened light, and made a chequered pavement of the great Broad Walk; "witch-elms did counter-change the floor" of the gravel-walks that wound with the windings of the Cherwell; the drooping willows were mirrored in its stream; through openings in the trees there were glimpses of grey old college buildings; then came the walk along the banks, the Isis[1] shining like molten silver, and fringed around with barges and boats; then another stretch of green meadows; then a cloud of steam from the railway-station; and a background of gently rising hills.'

And Dickens, writing to Angela Burdett-Coutts in 1856, says: 'Your letter from Oxford I received this morning. A beautiful place indeed! The rowing down from Oxford to Reading, on the Thames, is more charming than one can describe in words. I rowed down last June, through miles upon miles of water-lilies, lying on the water close together, like a fairy pavement.'

There are no miles of water-lilies now. Oxford is the first Thames town on the downstream route to pollute the river with effluents. The drainings of industry and sewage begin their insidious corruption here. The conveniences of flushing water-closets and industrially produced gas and electric power have shrivelled the lilies, and a lot of other aqueous life, into a watery grave.

As you will see when, later, I quote some findings of the Water Pollution Research Board, the Thames has considerable power to kill—and I don't mean only by drowning people

1. The classical name for the river, deriving from the Latin *Tamesis*, the broad Isis. Isis in this meaning has nothing to do with the Egyptian goddess of that name but is the Romans' adaptation of the words *esk*, *ouse*, and *uisg*, all meaning water, which words they found in use in Britain when they invaded. Until the eighteenth century the river was commonly called the Isis from its source all the way down to Dorchester, where it is joined by another river, confusingly called the Thame. But now only Oxford—very properly—sticks to the classical name.

F

who jump or fall into it. We still acknowledge the life-giving force of rivers by paying superstitious tribute to them. (A coin thrown in from Bablock Hythe ferry, a few miles west of Oxford, is supposed to return sevenfold.) But at the same time we gloomily contemplate the disastrous consequences of our apparently unalterable designs for death by pollution. This is of course a manifestation of the aspect of scientific discovery that results in both extending and exterminating life. Human and animal life are equally involved. But animal life has often had to fight for survival against human greed and ignorance, as well as against the achievements of science. From time to time this bothers people; and *anent* Oxford and the Thames I can tell you about one man who bothered more that I would have expected about the threatened extinction of one bit of animal life—the Thames salmon. This was King Henry the First of England.

5

Fire, Pyre, Flood and Frost

I

LIKE Alfred before him, Henry travelled up to Oxford from
Reading. But his transport was a royal barge, not a war-
ship. The medieval *Peterborough Chronicle* and other authorities seem to be divided about Henry's character, saying one
minute, 'Good man he was, peace he made for man and deer,
and there was great awe of him', and the next, 'Three gross
vices he had, greed and cruelty and wantonness'. But there's
no doubt that he liked pageantry and prayers. He founded
Reading Abbey specially to enable a new establishment of
monks from the Burgundian monastery of Cluny to pray for
him ('For the salvation of my soul,' he said in its Charter),
and he may well have felt he needed some praying for, since
he extorted money from rich and poor, ran red-hot needles
into the eyes of servants who offended him, and was completely merciless in quelling the risings of the peasantry.
Between risings, though, he seems to have been held in great
esteem, and everyone joined happily in the public occasions
in which he demonstrated his love of splendour.

The Oxford trip was one of these. He had recently returned from Rouen, where he had signed the foundation
charter of Reading Abbey, four years after laying the foundation stone in 1121, and he was anxious to carry the news
personally to the Franciscans who formed the nucleus of
scholarship that by the end of the century would lead to the
establishment of a university. Henry reigned before personal

arms and other heraldic devices had become conventional,
but there was no lack of colour about the trappings of his
kingship. On his barge his royal person was protected from
sun and rain by a jewel-encrusted scarlet canopy, and beneath
this were suspended curtains of cloth-of-gold emblazoned with
the blue fleurs-de-lis of France.

The barge was accompanied by outrider boats filled with
his personal bodyguard accoutred in armour and carrying
lances from which flew gonfalons embroidered with golden
lions. Their shields, shaped like fat exclamation marks, were
enamelled with blue and yellow rampant lions with scaly
coats. Henry's jester, Rahere, who had become so rich with
gifts from the king that he was able to endow St Bartholo-
mew's Hospital after his conversion to Christianity and entry
into a monastic order, acted as liaison with the Franciscans,
changing from his motley into monk's habit as the barge
approached the landing stage near where Folly Bridge crosses
the Thames today.

Disembarking after suitable trumpetings from the river
bank, Henry made his way to the castle preceded by his bodyguard and fifty gorgeously attired pages strewing flowers in
his path. Troubadors with lutes sang French love songs alongside the royal litter, and at the end of the procession monks
chanted endless litanies to keep at bay the subtle and envious
villains who might be expected to pursue the king because of
his royal grandeur.

At the castle he was feasted by the nobles and top citizenry
as a token of the city's somewhat belated respect for him.
(His father, William the Conqueror, had received nothing
but stubborn resistance from the Oxonians and had commanded his appointed governor, Robert D'Oyley, to impress
the finality of the conquest on the city by the erection of
impressive buildings—one of which was the castle he ordered
to be built on the site of the older fortifications.) The feast
included salmon caught on their way up the Thames to spawn,
and at the end of that course the king was asked if he would
be pleased to receive a humble deputation from the guild of

fishmongers. He agreed, and the cunning choice of time was soon evident. The fishmongers, after making sure that the salmon they had supplied had been approved of, pointed out that their trade was now in a parlous state because ignorant peasants were taking the fry—the tiny salmon, an inch or so long, that are the second stage of development after the hatching of the eggs—and feeding them to pigs. In a year or two, they gloomily predicted, there would be no salmon at all in the river because none would ever live to find their way downstream to the sea, grow, and return up the river to spawn. Henry listened, then wisely said that the fishmongers should wait while he considered the peasants' viewpoint too. The fishmongers bowed themselves out and the king sent messengers scurrying into the town to bring back peasants known to have fed their pigs on fry. Naturally this took some time, for by the time the messengers had traced the right sort of peasants the peasants had fled in terror, thinking they had incurred the king's displeasure and were bound to be punished.

The feast was long over and the king was preparing for his meeting with the Franciscans next day when a peasant named Gole was at last brought to the castle. Through an intermediary Gole explained that feeding fry to the pigs made them fat, and, since the root crops were poor in the area and Gole himself had nothing left over for swill after feeding his family he had taken fry from the river during the season because clearly they were too small to be of use to men and would be out of reach in the sea long before they had grown to worthwhile size. It says something for the king's patience and interest that he pointed out the shortsightedness of this policy, gave the peasant some coins, and sent him off with a royal blessing. He then sent for the fishmongers and told them that his wisdom had been grasped by at least one offending peasant and that that one would be so impressed that he would tell all the others. Doubtless a reasonable deduction, and doubtless the fry stealers toned down their activities considerably if not altogether.

But the impressiveness of an interview between a king and a peasant fades with the power of the peasant to talk about it, and less than a couple of hundred years later, in the reign of Edward III, a deputation from the fishmongers' guild was again calling on the king to present a petition seeking law to prevent farmers in the upper reaches of the Thames feeding fry to pigs. Evidently the fishmongers were again successful in finding a sympathetic listener, for salmon proliferated in the Thames until the end of the eighteenth century. After that their numbers steadily fell—unsurprisingly, for sewage was drained directly into the Thames soon after the invention of the flushing water-closet in 1810, and gas companies began the commercial production of gas for home and street lighting a few years later and expelled their waste products too into the river. The salmon had an ever diminishing chance of getting through the poisoned water. They gave up the battle about the middle of the century and haven't been seen since. All the same, Thames salmon might have been extinct seven hundred years earlier if Henry the First hadn't listened to the fishmongers during his feasting in the castle at Oxford.

Henry's daughter Matilda had a longer but less pleasant sojourn in the same castle in 1142. This was the result of the anarchistic reign of King Stephen. Both Matilda and Stephen were grandchildren of William the Conqueror, and both had been raised by Henry, whose maternal nephew Stephen was; but Stephen had sworn not to contest Matilda's right to the throne on Henry's death, and when he reneged on his promise and usurped the crown in 1135 he plunged England into a war of succession. There was no parliament or any other means by which the monarchy could be kept in check if it fell into evil or stupid hands. Stephen was not evil but he was stupidly romantic and completely inexperienced; he was quite unable to deal with the barons who were rebelling against the injustices heaped on them by Henry, and he weakly surrendered to the materialistic demands of the church. He and Matilda—who was equally unfit to rule—spent all their time raising armies to fight each other, largely by bribing influential barons and sheriffs with gifts of lands and charters of hereditary rule. Matilda actually reigned for a few months in 1141 while her temporarily superior forces kept Stephen prisoner; but the following year Stephen was king again and was pursuing his cousin into exile, he hoped.

In fact he pursued her only from London to Oxford, where she took refuge in the castle. Her army of squires and gallants swore to protect her from Stephen's attacks, and this they could easily do, because there weren't any. Advised by a brigand named Geoffrey de Mandeville, to whom he had given hereditary judiciary and administrative rights in Essex, Stephen besieged the castle by the much simpler process of cutting off its supplies of food and water. This was easy enough to arrange, for the castle was entirely dependent on outside sources. The head of the commissariat received merchants at the castle keep, gave them orders, and later received the grain, meat, and fish brought up by the merchants' serfs. His team of water carriers made daily journeys down to the Thames—which in those days flooded the entire area where now stand the railway stations, cattle market, recreation grounds, and cemetery—to refill the castle storage barrels. All Stephen had to do was to ambush the serfs, and this he did courteously, transferring them and their supplies over the ford to his camp on the south side of the river. Some supplies got in from the north through gaps in Stephen's ambuscade, but gradually Matilda and her supporters were starved out. Several of her officers unchivalrously but understandably walked deliberately into ambush so that they could at least get prisoners' rations; and Matilda herself 'grew lean and weary of the want and emptiness of the granary, and no succour was anywhere'.

It was winter, bitterly cold, and it says a good deal for Matilda's determination and physical toughness that she managed to hold out for over two months before thinking of surrender.

By this time the U of river and the extensive marshes west of the town had frozen over; the town was no longer cut off on three sides by its moat. The ford on the south side, previously the only crossing, was no longer important; the river could be crossed anywhere on the thick ice. Stephen had only the small army that was necessary for use in ambuscade; he could not possibly surround the town. But he could move his troops in across the ice and surround the castle, and this he did—at the same time exposing them to battle with Matilda's defenders. There were some brief clashes which ended in the defeat of the queen's unnourished troops, and Stephen entered the castle. There was a church adjoining it and Matilda sought sanctuary there with her attendants while Stephen's men searched the halls and bashed at the doors. By nightfall they had still not discovered her and they postponed further search till the morning.

Stephen, though no ruler, was a man of knightly chivalry and most probably felt inclined to give his rival a fair chance to escape. The popular story is that Matilda was lowered from the tower of the castle by ropes, but it is much more likely that when night had fallen she simply emerged from the church, made her way unhindered across the frozen marshes to the Thames, crossed, and walked on to Abingdon. At all events she escaped—and none too soon, for during the night a quick thaw restored the river and marshes to their normal state. Matilda, hearing of this, made in gratitude a gift of money to 'people living about the river to be used for wine and comfort them in cold'.

II

People living about the river, whether warmed by gift wine like Matilda's or not, acquire special characteristics in the course of time and genetic development. They develop, for one thing, a wariness towards the possibilities of flooding— just as mining villagers are attuned to the sounds of disaster and mountain villagers know the turns in the weather that may bring the avalanche. Like rustics tolerant of the summer storm that flattens the barley, they learn to be longanimous, to look more or less serenely over the river that needs no more than a winter's snow and sudden thaw to make it swell and come pouring into their sitting-rooms. Unlike, for instance, London workers who commute from the suburbs and sit by the Thames in grateful wonder eating luncheon sandwiches, or townee motorists who decorate their lives with synthetic romance by ambling along a towpath, riverside dwellers accept, rather than consciously enjoy, their rivers. The beady eye of wariness is a corrective. The Old Father Thames attitude was neatly put in its place by a bargee I know who referred to the Thames *en passant* as 'this stinking bastard bloody river'.

The Thames certainly became stinking at its estuary end during the nineteenth century, and from time to time it has been literally bloody—though hardly to the extent that Macbeth saw the multitudinous seas incarnadined by his murderous hand. The grimmest of such occasions seems to have been in 1355, when there was a riot that typified the acrimonious spirit abounding in Oxford in those days.

Basically this conflict was between church and peasantry, between scholarly privilege and selfconscious ignorance, and between Jews and Gentiles—all represented by belligerent factions. At this distance of time it is impossible to sort out the varying degrees of responsibility, but the story-line is this :

Students whose family backgrounds and wealth enabled them to aim at becoming scholars went, until the middle of the twelfth century, to the University of Paris, France's influence in learning being as strong as in everything else after the conquest. Henry the Second's French wars, however, resulted in students being expelled and deported back to England. Henry, a man of almost schizophrenic division of temperament, responded with one of his furious outbursts of anger and forbade students to leave England at all for their education. The crown's close connexion with the Franciscan scholars at Oxford drew students to the town, and although there was no officially recognised centre of learning there, it was now that the nucleus of one began to form. Students boarded in the riverside houses—hovels, really—of the peasants and attended daily lectures given by monks and guilded teachers.

At first they only listened and were not required to be examined to see whether any of the golden words had sunk in. But gradually a system of responsive teaching came into being. The branches of study were grouped together as the *trivium* of rhetoric, dialectic, and grammar, and the *quadrivium* of astronomy, music, geometry, and arithmetic, plus natural, moral, and metaphysical philosophies. Four years of study brought the student to the point at which he was called upon as a disputant in a public *viva voce* and gained a bachelor's degree if sharp enough in debate. After three more years he was received as a 'master' if he had the right referees to commend him to the chancellor. He then chose a faculty and continued his studies in medicine, law, or theology.

The evolution of this system took more than a century, and one of its results was the schism between scholarship and commerce. I don't mean commerce in the sense of industrial progress (Oxford remained non-industrial until the twentieth century), but, rather, the sort of commerce that concerns itself with rents and living accommodation. There had been an influx of Jews who, with their racial shrewdness, had foreseen the increasing need for student lodgings and had built themselves houses which they let on terms that were profitable but sometimes seemed rapacious to the students who boarded in them.

This in turn resulted in the building by students of their own hostels where they could live simply and cheaply. In this way resentment was born, and nothing was easier than its nourishment. Rivalries feed on acrimony, and before long the Jewish landlords—many of whom had become town burgesses—were laying complaints against the unruly behaviour of the students. In this they were justified, for the students were not only unruly but were also given to persecutionary practices—including the masked holdup of Jews and their subsequent humiliation by ducking in the Thames. By the end of the thirteenth century peasantry and townsmen were square against friars and students, and this town-gown bitterness built up to an affray in 1298 when two scholars were arrested for drunkenness and for three days there was partisan fighting in the streets as a result.

It was recorded by one of the scriveners employed by the friars to write up this affray that no cleric was safe and that there were rumours of a general uprising throughout the shire. For the time being, however, this came to nothing. An appeal was made to the king—he was Edward the First—by the sheriff, but Edward had more onerous troubles to contend with than street fighting in Oxford. He had William Wallace and Robert Bruce revolting against his kingship of Scotland, Margaret of France being difficult about his courtship of her, and his chancellor continually reminding him of his financial embarrassment. But, influenced by the fact that John Balliol, the contender for the throne of Scotland favoured by Edward in the dispute in which he had acted as arbiter in 1292, had founded a living for Oxford scholars, he strengthened the powers of the university by enacting a law that made the persons of students and lay teachers as untouchably sacred as those of the clerics. At a time when the country was in any case heading gradually towards the national uprising of 1381 this imposition was by no means well received. For over fifty years it irritated the town-gown relationship, which by 1355 had become an inflamed sore ready to erupt again.

As before, a couple of drunks began the trouble. Ironically, they were not representatives of opposing factions; both were peasants, and their brawl started for God knows what incoherent reason. But it gathered a crowd that was far from incoherent and was soon reinforcing opposing opinions with physical violence. By nightfall flaming torches illuminated scenes of increasing disorder. Narrow lanes were filled with a populace who were unled and uncommitted except to brutality, lust, and pillage. The houses of the rich were looted and the daughters of peasants raped in their hovels. The city walls resounded with screams of pain and were lit by flaming effigies. Corpses were decapitated, veins opened, and blood drunk in mockery of the eucharist. Untrammelled frenzy continued through the night, but when morning came there was no real respite. The dead and exhausted were replaced by an influx of people from outside the city and these were fresh with purpose and lost no time in organising the rabble of peasants into a formidable ripieno to swell the townsmen's orchestra of anger.

The students, for their part, also quickly organised themselves into a unified assembly with battle leaders and some glimmerings of strategy in their plans. For a few hours a sullen silence filled the city. The friars prayed and the burgesses sent urgent messages to Wallingford, where troops were garrisoned. The messengers, however, were ambushed by students and their beaten up bodies thrown into the Thames. At dusk a party of students made their way by a circuitous route outside the city wall down to the river and there fired a store full of casks of lamp oil.

Within a few minutes the store collapsed and the flaming oil fell upon the river. Hovels, boats, and the timber causeway over the marshes connecting the river with the castle moat were consumed by the holocaust, which raged for an hour, blackened the city walls, and left a scum of thick ash on the water. But this was only the beginning. Homeless peasants rallied to the burgesses' call and began to sack all the students' hostels and town houses that had escaped the previous day's fracas. Students, guild teachers, and faculty masters were butchered as the townees came upon them mustering in alleys. Knives and clubs slit and smashed into flesh, High Street flamed and stank with burning bodies and echoed to the yells of the mob. Half a dozen Jewish landlords trying to escape westward across the marshes were pursued by a violent horde, caught, stripped naked, strung by the feet from trees and disembowelled alive while their viscera were roasted on the fires that had been built beneath them.

At last the monks, who had prudently sheltered themselves

in the castle or within the thick walls of their friaries, decided to bring the invoked power of God to bear. The spiritual power of the church, they thought, would be enough to quieten things down if they went in procession through the city threatening excommunication. The threat had its practical value, for the church owned most of the land, and excommunication meant that the common man's means of livelihood—his cultivation of a designated acreage of land—was pulled from beneath his feet.

As the news of the monks' processional approach filtered through to the mob there was a slight but general abatement of anger. Even in the midst of a massacre the threat had its effect. But it was only a temporary effect. The temperature of extreme violence was not to be lowered by awe. The procession of monks headed by the crucifix would normally have passed through respectful ranks of genuflecting citizens. But now only the students and scholars made their obeisances. As they did so they were set upon by the townsmen and peasants. For twenty-four hours now the population had been swelled by an influx of people from all directions and far away who rode, marched, and rampaged into the city inflamed by the news that there was a battle to be joined and who immediately joined it—naturally on the winning side of the townsmen—and these, added to the already swollen population, were in a proportion of about one hundred to one of the representatives of church and university. The procession of monks was scarcely more than a few hundred yards on its way south through the city when it was set upon. I could discover no record of the number of monks in the procession, but fifty or sixty seems a probable number. However many there were they were knifed, clubbed, kicked, and beaten. The scholars who bravely but feebly tried to defend them were treated with similar mercilessness and together with the monks were forced down through the narrow streets towards the river. The still smoking remains of the fired houses were blown once more into flame and in the lurid light the monks were tortured severally and collectively, some being hacked to pieces, others thrown live onto the flames like logs being added to a funeral pyre. The river banks were strewn with corpses and hacked-off limbs were thrown into the water. 'The river ran with blood', a chronicler says; and since mutilation, decapitation, and the tearing out of hearts and guts seems to have been the order of the day, his phrase may not be quite the hyperbole it seems.

The end of the story was that the remaining scholars fled the city, the interlopers who had reinforced the townsmen and peasants returned to their homes in the surrounding country, and the Oxonians set about restoring some order—one hopes with a feeling of remorse, but it seems doubtful. By now the news of the riot had reached Wallingford and troops were sent to arrest the ringleaders. Since there weren't any who could be certainly identified the troops arrested an assortment of two hundred townsmen and peasants and a report was sent to the king. He dismissed the sheriff, put an interdict on the town, approved a penitential interdict imposed by the Archbishop of Canterbury, and gave the university a new charter that made its chancellor virtually dictator of the town. The river bore its grisly mementos of the riot eastward, and weakened the violently spilled blood of a few human bodies to invisibility.

III

That wariness I mentioned—the unease with which riverside dwellers look upon their aeonian companion—is understandable. The difference in disastrous consequences to those living in the valleys of the Mississippi and the Thames is only one of magnitude. When the Mississippi choked itself with the great rains of February to July, 1928, it flooded an area of twenty-nine thousand square miles, and up to the time of writing this event still ranks as the greatest meteorological calamity of the twentieth century. When in January of the same year the Thames rose to its highest possible level because a storm surge in the North Sea forced the tidal waters back up the estuary, fourteen people were drowned. The Mississippi claimed half a million and made another half million homeless. But there would be little distinction calamity-wise in the minds of the two sets of victims.

Dwellers on the actual river banks are not, of course, the only people in trouble at flood times. Tumultuous washes of rainwater down the valley sides take all before them, including crops and topsoil; and though soil erosion is no great problem in the Thames valley it isn't altogether to be disregarded. The Ministry of Agriculture in one of its publications gloomily predicts, 'During the ensuing year a minimal loss of 27.83 acres due to erosive effects is to be expected.' But the greatest predictable danger for Thames valley residents is from the rapid thawing of prolonged snow following a biting frost. The ground is made by the frost as impenetrable as if encased in an iron jerkin a foot thick, thousands upon thousands of tons of water pile up on the surface in the crystalline form of snow and, melted by sudden warmth, pour down the valley sides over the non-absorbent earth, and inevitable disaster follows.

However, it is one of the more cheering of humanity's traits that predictable disasters are often met with determined if feeble efforts to avert them. The more ludicrously feeble such efforts are, the more cheering they seem when they meet with some measure of success. As for instance on an occasion I should never have learnt about but for my occasional serendipity, which brought about my meeting with Lindo Mortifor. Mr Mortifor, an attendant at a filling station where Willie Hyne topped up the tank of his Amphicar while he was driving me round and about Oxford, took a mordant view of writers. (It was of course Willie Hyne who told him I was a writer, in the usual tone of people who are temporarily saddled with one and, assuming him to be odd, haven't yet determined whether he is odd-contemptible or odd-enviable. It is the tone of someone introducing an acquaintance who has at some time rated a short paragraph in the local paper recording an arrest for indecent exposure.) Mr Mortifor, difficult to put into a definite age-group, had springy white hair which he was continually trouncing with the flat of his hand and a rhinophymous nose. His mordant view was expressed and explained as follows. (I am reporting with as much accuracy as the treacheries of memory allow. My desire to be efficient was as usual ahead of my capacity to be so; and my pen was inkless.)

'A writer, are you? Sort of stuff you write?'

'Reportage, I suppose you'd call it. At the moment I'm nosing into various aspects of the Thames.'

'Writers are a bind to me.'

'They are to many people. Have you ever had any conversation with writers' wives?'

' 'Tisn't that. Too much writing—that's their trouble. The library told me—twenty-four thousand books published last year. Last year alone. You can't keep up. Some of those are my sorta book—history, g'ography, biography, all that stuff. Too much of it says the same thing again. You reckon anyone wants to read another book about the Thames?'

'You never know,' I said with the false cheeriness of a man whistling in the threatening dark. 'My own experience is that not many people read any books about anything.'

'Where's all those books go, then? No good you talking in that hyperbowl. You must know they get read, some of them, somewhere. Look at Australia. People there hungry for books, the library tells me. And they know. But too many about the same things, that's the trouble. You really writing a book about the Thames?'

'Yes,' I said.

He paused to return the pump nozzle to its hook, collect the money, and ineffectually smite his hair into place again. Then he came back to the car.

'All right, then. I've got something might be interesting. Anyway, you probably wouldn't know about it without someone told you. I've got a book, one of those privately printed ones, sixteen-fifty-three the date is—and it isn't smut just because it's private printed—with some stuff about the great flood in it. You want to see it?'

Of course I wanted to see it. I wanted to see everything. I arranged to go to Mr Mortifor's that evening after he'd finished his stint at the garage. His house—a small one jammed between two terraces of Victorian stuccoed villas—contained plenty of reasons for his bewildered and tetchy attitude towards literature. He told me he had fifteen thousand books. I should have put the figure higher. They were piled and shelved in every room except the kitchen (which was also the bathroom). His small camp bed was surrounded with crenellated walls of books. Towers of books trembled as traffic whizzed past the house. He told me to sit on his bed while he found the book he'd suggested might be helpful. It took him about two minutes and I can only suppose that one of his characteristics was an indexed memory. It was a thin book bound in crumbling leather and its title page said it was *The Revelacions of Sidney Gilliham, Gent., To The Interested Publick*. While I read in it and made notes Mr Mortifor wound his way through the books to the kitchen to prepare 'a snack'. (Surprisingly, the snack, when it was served, turned out to be Parma ham with melon, and Thames trout, grilled. It was entirely delicious.)

Gilliham's revelations were for the most part trivial and of devastating dullness. But there were half a dozen pages that I found revealing about the Thames. They recorded 'the disasterous flooding' of spring, 1595, which Gilliham recalled from his boyhood days.

He lived in St Aldate's, which is the street running due north through the old city of Oxford from Folly Bridge, and his father, a mercer, had lived there before him and like everyone in Oxford was well used to the inundations made by the rivers that embraced the city. Tales of cattle lost, homes flooded, and people drowned were traditional and had been glossed with details that were the decorations of dead-pan narrators talking to credulous listeners—the folklore of centuries. Gilliham senior had known them all—including an

G

improbable tale of a pig who had hurled himself into a breach in a hastily built embankment and delayed the river's bursting waters long enough for an exodus from endangered huts, which sounds to me suspiciously like a crib from the one about the Dutch boy with his finger in the dyke—and had apparently entertained his son with them at bedtime. But Gilliham junior simply used them as a buildup to his personal experience in 1593.

That year the whole of the shire was in the grip of a black and bitter frost for two months before Christmas, 1592, and unceasing snow from the 23rd December to 31st March following. 'My father took me walking,' Gilliham wrote, 'and showed to me the bodies of beggars frozen to death in their verie walking, beside the roads to the south and to east and west and north they were dead, five wee counted, and my father made this a lesson for mee to learn the five times table. The dead bodies of birds also fell from the trees and foxes abandoned their wily ways and came exhausted into houses to be fed, but were themselves eaten, so little was there and so hard to get in these cold days.'

Drifts of snow threatened at times to bury the city; only the diligent digging of relays of increasingly exhausted men kept houses visible at all. In those in which people had been too poor or too improvident to store wood and consequently had no fires, roofs collapsed with the weight of unmelted snow upon them—'It was a great silent world in which only the creeking of timbers could be heard.' As is usual with the English, the apparent attitude to the weather combined irritable comment ('Dreadful weather we're having') with phlegmatic resignation ('Nothing we can do about it'). But there was a great deal of underlying concern about the eventual thaw. Prayers were said in the churches for 'a reasonable and equitable lifting of the winter that wee may not all bee flooded for our sins which wee acknowledge and will repent'. The Thames, frozen, according to Gilliham, 'God knoweth how far to the west and to the east to Wallingford and beyond', was of course the greatest threat. (It was also the only means of communication, all roads being snowbound, and wagons and pedestrians crowded its solidly frozen crust.)

The snow continued to fall and the weeks to pass and among the university faculty of scientists there were gloomy prognostications that even the earth itself might cave in with the great weight lying upon it. More commercially minded prophets sold charms against drowning and broadsheets of prayers claimed to be specially written 'for reliefs from whatever might befall if the warm cometh quickly and we are undone', while astrologers were busier than doctors. The town-versus-gown enmity had never quite died (it still hasn't today) but such hatchets as were unsheathed were buried in the snow and every brain was racked for ideas that might forestall or mitigate disaster.

Gilliham records some of the odd ones that were suggested : great fires dotting the countryside and melting the snow as it fell; pipes pushed through the snow and filled with a constant supply of hot water poured in by relays of workers; great stretches of ice to be cut from the river and the snow dumped therein; and similar demonstrations of impractical ingenuity. Apart from this direct approach the help of alleged wizards and witches was enlisted, and many of them were so convincing in their assurance of the power of spells that they were given written assurances of freedom from persecution. But in the end it was neither crackpottery nor spellbinding that helped to save the day.

Astrologers and other wise birds forecast that the break in the weather would come in April (a fairly safe prophecy, one would have thought, even in England); and indeed by the last week in March something of the bleakness had gone from the weather. Snow continued to fall from uniformly grey stretches of cloud and the wind remained piercing; but there was an intangible 'lightening of the temperature which no gage reveals but all felt as a prescience of the coming thaw'. Terrified of coming floods people began to leave the city, travelling mainly southward to Abingdon. Many roofs had collapsed and the loss of cattle and domestic goats had been cruel. If the thaw was rapid 'the entire city would be drowned', Gilliham heard from some source he evidently thought to be authoritative. The mayor and sheriff went into consultation, announced that they had discarded all the ideas presented and called upon the citizens to begin to erect flood barriers along the river bank 'so soon as the snows begin their melting'. What the flood barriers were to be made of they didn't specify; but the only thing of any use was the local stone. 'A thousand men', Gilliham says, 'were day and night uncovering the quarries and then hewing the stone therefrom, which they passed by chain and wagon and whatever means they could to the Isis. In this way, with others clearing snow but barely faster than it fell, from the meadows and marshes, a wall was crudely built. Full of cracks for lack of time to join the stones in proper measure, but solid to the ground and impossible to fall though a great burden be placed against it.'

This was an optimistic view; but in the event, ludicrously frail against such an enormous pressure though the wall was, it helped. And one cannot but admire the stoicism of men who achieved the task of quarrying first the snow and ice and then the stone from the ironclad country. It was a wall uneven in height as in every other facet of its construction, and it had gaps 'big enough for a small man to come through'. But when the rapid thaw began—which it did on the eighth day of April —it delayed the swollen waters for a while, like the alleged pig that so nobly hurled itself into the breach.

Even so the flood was, as Gilliham says, 'disasterous'. Christ Church Meadow was under 'thirteen foot of water, and in High Street and Saint Aldate's it was scarcely less, my own house revealing only its upper rooms (which we contrived to live in a while until a burgess of the town and my father's friend made rescue of us in a boat and took us to his friend's house above Banbury, where the flood had not reached). We returned only when two months were out and the waters had abated, but had taken with it great toll of life both human and cattle, viz: it is said that more than an hundred were drowned and an hundred more dead of maladies brought by the waters, besides the dead animals lying in scores upon the ground after the waters returned to their proper course. And likewise all houses in the lower and upper rooms were spoilt and all within ruined, so that those coming back were without beds or even pans for cooking; and green slime and fungus on the walls where curtains hung before and logs and candles made all bright. My father did abandon the house and we stayed at an hostelrie the while it was baled and dried with great fires, all of which took some months, and I cannot remember that we were back within the year. And no such flood have I known since, and I thank God for it. But this one I remember.'

Understandably. Oxford's riverside has been flooded occasionally even since the marshes were drained and cuts provided, but the floods have not, so far as I could discover, inundated high enough to drown the houses in St Aldate's. In 1947, though, after the thaw following another bitter winter, Christ Church Meadow was flooded eight feet deep and when the water receded an unaccountable drowned cow was revealed (unaccountable because the cows normally grazing there had all been stored in their byres when the winter set in). It isn't surprising that the ingrained memories of such overpourings of the river lead to a certain apprehensive cynicism in the dwellers on or near it.

IV

All the same, my experience was that Oxonians demonstrate, when necessary, a stronger affection for their river than almost anyone else along its banks. They are militant with indignation as soon as any upstart suggests a plan that might involve interference with its form or character. In 1959, for example, during one of the periodical revivals of the controversy between Town and Gown about whether or not a by-pass road should be built through Christ Church Meadow,

an over-enthusiastic planner suggested that if the traditional-
ists didn't want to run a road through their meadow it would
be quite possible to divert the Thames along a completely new
course and build the road along the present river bed. The
resulting cries of anguish left no doubt about Oxonians' unity
in their hands-off-the-river attitude, even if they were at
loggerheads regarding the respective claims of progress and
tradition in the city itself. One lady actually admonished the
plan's proposer at a public meeting with the words 'How dare
you, sir!', while similarly exclamatory Blimpisms were
bandied about in the press. Ridiculous though such outbursts
may seem, they represented a very strong feeling that Oxonians would go to any length in defence of their Thames against
interference, however much trouble the river may have
caused them in the past (and probably would in the future).

This feeling seemingly does not reveal itself strongly unless
there is a real threat to the river. At least, that was my impression. I talked to a number of people on and near the Oxford
bank and their indifference to it seemed marked. 'Well, it's
just a river, isn't it?' was a common comment. Several people
in north Oxford said that though they'd lived there for years
they'd never so much as been down to the river. But when I
asked them if they remembered the 1959 furore and, if so,
which side they were on, most of them replied to the effect
that Yes indeed they remembered, and naturally they were
against interference with the river. Except in one case, though,
I didn't detect any enthusiasm behind the 'naturally'.

The exception was a man who said : 'Well, you don't have
to swim in the thing or picnic on its bloody banks to raise
your voice when somebody wants to muck about with it, do
you? I've never been down that far'—the Thames, by the
way, is one mile, a brisk fifteen minutes' walk, from this man's
home on the Woodstock Road—'but there's plenty of places
I've never been to I've got opinions about. There's too much
of this "couldn't care less" feeling about nowadays. People
ought to have opinions about things, give shout to 'em too.
Getting like a lot of bloody sheep, we are.' But, as I say, there

was only this one man who displayed so strongly his resentment towards interference with a Thames he'd never seen. Affection or regard for the river is in general effectively disguised beneath indifference and even active hostility until a real threat causes hackles to rise.

One public figure who was an exemplar of just such an ambivalent relationship was William Morris, Lord Nuffield, who, as I said earlier, turned the village of Cowley into a sprawling suburb of Oxford in the 1920s.

Morris was born in 1877 in Worcester, but he was educated—not very well—in Cowley and adopted the place wholeheartedly. Like many self-made men he warded off criticism with philanthropy of the easy kind and concealed his witlessness and lack of sophistication behind a carapace of malevolence. His eventual biographer, Robert Jackson, was threatened with unremitting legal action when he sought collaboration during Nuffield's lifetime—though when the biography appeared in 1964 it proved to be painstakingly honest and failed in its objectivity only in lacunae that could easily have been bridged to Nuffield's advantage by his co-operation. He was a vindictive man who harboured injuries for years; but he was also a philanthropist in the true sense of beaming goodwill towards those who served him well, and the welfare of his staff was never neglected. Many of his stealthier kindnesses were revealed to me when I rounded up a number of people whom I wanted to talk to because they were Thames-side dwellers who chanced also to be life-long employees of the Morris organisation—which now, by the way, is a division of the even vaster British Motor Corporation. But I'm concerned with Morris as a Thames man rather than a benefactor, stealthy or otherwise, and it was that aspect of him that I probed my captives about.

When he worked in his bicycle shop in Oxford before the first world war, Morris tried out several of his experimental motor-cycles and cars along the towing path on the south bank of the river. He chose this testing ground to get away from the prying eyes of putative filchers of his ideas and also from the representatives of Gownsmanship, who could be particularly tiresome on the subject of the internal combustion engine. (Their continuing pretence that the city needs no adjustment to accommodate this demon of the twentieth century has resulted in worse traffic snarl-ups than even those in Reading, which is saying something.)

According to one of my informants, it was during an interval between tests that Morris sat on one of the towing-path seats and thumbed through an old magazine that had an advertisement for an American car in it—the 1905 Winton —and decided that motoring would never become popular in Britain until we did what Henry Ford had done and made it cheaper. The Winton was indeed a luxury car and in 1905 cost $4,500 with a limousine body. (It also had, according to the catalogue I managed to root out, 'four upright cylinders, fed by one single gas-mixer, and fired by one single magneto . . . new patented Steering Gear . . . Safest, surest, simplest speed-control . . . dashing style . . . twin springs . . . long, graceful lines, sidedoor entrance', and could be 'run by a youth, after one hour's coaching'.) Morris didn't have to think very hard to see that if he could emulate Ford and take the motor-car out of the realm of luxury and give a mass-produced model a British trademark he would be made.

'Later on,' my informant said, 'feature writers used to perpetuate the shocking lie that the Guv'nor—Sir or Guv'nor, he wouldn't be called anything else—had his inspiration at that moment. He's supposed to have got up, waved this magazine about, looked at the river, which was very high after a long spell of rainy weather, and shouted out, "There is a tide in the affairs of men, which, taken at the flood, leads on to fortune". As you're a literary man you'll know that's a bit from *Julius Caesar*. And I can assure you that the Guv'nor no more knew a line of Shakespeare than he could fly in the air. But it's the sort of picturesque thing these chaps like to get hold of, and once it's invented it's very hard to kill—not that he ever tried very hard to kill it, I don't think. It gave him a bit of a cachet, you see? But in any case,

there wasn't much inspiration about his work: he was a practical man, not a theorist.

'I doubt if he could ever in his life have explained the
theory of internal combustion; but he could do anything with
the tools of his trade. And it is true that he thought of the
Thames with affection because of his memory of test runs
along the bank. He chartered a pleasure steamer several times
to take the children of employees on a two-day trip down as
far as Reading and back—mine were included, so I know
—and he used to point out the stretch of bank he used for
test runs and for pacing himself in the bike races he used to
win so many trophies in.

'But after he built up the works at Cowley in the twenties
he used to get all the blame for making Oxford vulgar and
for polluting the river with the outfall from the plant. He
used to say "What the hell's the damn river for if it's not to
take muck down to the sea?" All the same, when the first
by-pass roads were planned in nineteen-twenty-seven, the
Guv'nor saw the river was threatened and stirred up so much
opposition that the roads, as you know, have never been done.
Mind you, he took the other view when he saw Oxford was
getting choked with traffic, which he was adding to at the
rate of fifty thousand cars a year; but it was always the plan
that didn't involve Christ Church Meadow or the river that
he favoured. As things have turned out, though, the whole
road problem's got into a complete knot, and I can't see it
being untied in our lifetime. So the river's likely to be left
alone, and I think the Guv'nor would approve of that.'

What Nuffield didn't really approve of was education in
the broad sense. He endowed Nuffield College but never
really forgave the authorities for refusing to let it specialise
in science. The College became the dispersal point for the
wisdom of such distinguished men as the historian Professor
Max Beloff, and Nuffield's views on history were on all fours
with Henry Ford's. He is reported, in a eulogistic essay written
by an approved henchman, as having found an under-
graduate poring over a study book in Christ Church Meadow

one afternoon and of having taken him by the elbow and
thrust him down to the river's edge to say irritably:

'Philosophy, history, trigonometry, religion—you can't take
it *all* in. Look at that river and keep to one course as *it* does
and you'll get there in the end.'

The student's response to this pearl of wisdom is, perhaps
wisely, unrecorded; but Nuffield's alleged utterance is just
one of innumerable inspirational bromides the Thames has
been saddled with. Lyric poets have been much given to
gushing about it, perhaps in a sense justifiably. But Francis
Thompson gets the apocalyptic twitches ('And lo, Christ
walking on the water/Not of Gennesareth, but Thames');
William Morris (the earlier one) hokes up a London that
never was ('. . . dream of London, small and white and clean/
The clear Thames bordered by its gardens green'); Ben
Jonson drools about a most un-Shakespearean Shakespeare
('Sweet Swan of Avon . . ./. . . make those flights upon the
banks of Thames,/that so did take Eliza, and our James!');
Bridges sets a picture-postcard scene ('There is a hill beside
the silver Thames/Shady with birch and Beech and odorous
pine'); Arnold nods himself into a pleonastic doze ('Crossing
the stripling Thames at Babcock Hythe/Trailing in the cool
stream thy fingers wet'); and many a pageant producer has
depicted the river in the most improbable symbolic forms—
perhaps taking their cue from John Crowne, whose *Calisto*
demands in its stage directions 'River Thames, attended by
two nymphs, representing Peace and Plenty'. (I hope I've
said enough to convince you that peace and plenty do not
typify the river's character.)

Some writers have of course found the Thames of more
practical value. Richard Lovelace thought of it as a hangover
cure ('When flowing cups run swiftly round/With no allaying
Thames'); Horace Walpole saw it as a merciful barrier when
he wrote 'Thank God! the Thames is between me and the
Duchess of Queensbury'; and the number of novelists who
have dumped murdered bodies in it, joined heroes and hero-
ines in gooey romance on it, let their suicides leap into it, and

used it as narrative linkage, are beyond computation. The most famous Thames novelist is Jerome K. Jerome (the K stands for Klapka), whose *Three Men in a Boat* set out to be a serious historical and topographical account of the river but ended up as a famous funny book. Topography and history are limited to guide-book comments. ('From Abingdon to Nuneham Courtenay is a lovely stretch. Nuneham Park is well worth a visit. It can be viewed on Tuesdays and Thursdays. The house contains a fine collection of pictures, and the grounds are very beautiful.') But Jerome can be trusted to see the only bit of marmoreally remarkable but quite useless information in a church ('In St Helen's Church [Abingdon], it is recorded that W. Lee, who died in 1637, "had in his lifetime issue from his loins two hundred lacking but three" '). And he can be a heady evoker of the miseries of river transport in the rain : 'The river—chill and weary, with the ceaseless raindrops falling on its brown and sluggish waters, with the sound as of a woman, weeping low as in some dark chamber, while the woods, all dark and silent, shrouded in their mists of vapour, stand like ghosts upon the margin; silent ghosts with eyes reproachful, like the ghosts of evil actions, like the ghosts of friends neglected—is a spirit-haunted water through the land of vain regrets.' After enduring just such depressing weather for two days during their journey downstream from Oxford, Jerome and his companions reneged on their decision to have a fortnight's trip on the river if it killed them, caught a London train at Pangbourne, and went to the Alhambra. I was reminded of them when it came to my time to leave Oxford.

v

There were depressing signs of twenty-four hours of drenching rain to come as I settled my score with Willie Hyne, thanked him for the amphibious convenience afforded by his Amphicar and his captaincy, and prepared to tramp downstream as far as Abingdon—a distance of about eight miles. I have a stubborn disbelief in the forecasts of the Meteorological Office, and prefer to rely on adages like 'rain before seven, clear before eleven' (which I always stumble over because I never seem to know whether G.M.T. or B.S.T. is in operation) and 'red sky at dawning, shepherd's warning'; and since there had been a flaming dawn sky and the rain had started at 8.30 I had my reasons for doubting the forecast on the wireless, which had promised a cool dry day with some sunshine and a light southerly wind. I had enveloped myself in my plastic mac and was crossing the footbridge by the gas works when I weakly decided that an eight-mile walk along a wet towing path would probably kill me and would certainly drown my words, either eventually meaning the end of this book before I'd completed it. I sped along to Salter's Boat House by Folly Bridge and was fortunate in my timing. One of their pleasure steamers was leaving in an hour. I got aboard it and sheltered in the saloon with a handful of passengers all making the usual comments about the weather in the indignant tone we English use when analysing the promise of the previous three days compared with the achievement of the day we're actually living in. ('I saw those mackerel clouds Tuesday night, and when there was that clear dew Wednesday morning and the mackerels again last night I thought, "We're in for a fine spell." I said it to the wife. I said, "We're in for a fine spell, let's go on a Salter's, it'll be nice." And now look at it.')

Salter Brothers have been building pleasure boats at Oxford for the best part of a hundred years now. Except for breaks during the war years, these steamers have steamed up and down the Thames between Oxford and Kingston every summer weekday at the same times since before the beginning of the century. The timetable for 1900 says:

'The through journey from Oxford to Kingston can be made in two days by the morning Steamer. The Steamer stops the night *en route* at Henley.

'The fares do not include Hotel accommodation, for which passengers make their own arrangements.

'Passengers can join or leave the boat at any of the locks or regular stopping places, and holders of through tickets may break their journey at these places and resume it by a later boat.

'Light refreshments are supplied on board, and arrangements have been made for Luncheons at 2/6 each to be ready on arrival of the Steamers each day at Wallingford, Henley, Windsor and Kingston.

'A dark room is provided in the boat for the use of Photographers. No dogs allowed on board.'

If you can forget the rise in prices of fares and Light Refreshments the Salter world is practically unchanged today. The steamers carry in, and on top of, their plush, mahogany, and brass saloons aft, and under the striped awning forward of the central funnel, two-hundred-plus passengers in seated comfort. (Easily four times that number could be herded aboard, but since 1878, when the *Princess Alice* sank at Greenwich and six hundred and forty people sank with her—a disaster I shall tell about in due course—the number of trippers per steamer has been restricted.) The prevailing ambience aboard is of endless leisure, pre-1914 expansiveness in matters of time. Rupert Brooke's Grantchester reverie on the church clock standing still at ten to three might well have been written aboard one of Salter's steamers.

They propel themselves with the indifferent doziness of reminiscing prima donnas between the shores of a world where the luncheon is still ready at Wallingford, Henley, Windsor, and Kingston, but 2/6 nowadays will just about tip the cloakroom attendant. No-one has seen fit to alter the schedule; and although today as in 1900 the timetable carries a warning that 'Approximate times are given, punctuality is not guaranteed', no-one I spoke to could remember a Salter steamer being late.

Not surprisingly, dramas aboard these tranquillising vessels are rare. Those I was able to fish up from the secreting river were, in descending order of magnitude, as follows: A jilted photographer, having developed in the boat's dark room the evidential picture of his perfidious girl-friend in a clinch with his rival, transfixed the film and a celluloid developer dish with a hatpin, opened his wrists, and was found in a welter of blood and hypo-sulphite half an hour later. Fifteen years went by and drama struck again. This time it was a happy drunk who attempted the Lovelace hangover cure of jumping into the 'allaying Thames'. I looked up the *Berkshire Observer* expecting to find in its report some such coyly chuckling headline as 'inebriated person of no fixed address finds abode in river'; but the incident turned out to rate a furious outburst on 'A Disgraceful Exhibition Aboard A Pleasure Steamer'. The exhibitionist was a cobbler from Armagh, but no-one explained how he came to be cruising drunkenly down the Thames. He was rescued by line and lifebelt and appeared in court next day to be fined £2 and given a harsh talking-to by the magistrate, who said his behaviour was 'beastly'. Only six months later (this was 1913, the richest year for Thames steamer excitement) the violinist of 'a small string band playing selections from *Floradora* for the entertainment of passengers' was 'lacerated about the face by a sudden hailstorm in which sharp-edged stones as big as hen eggs were picked up'. After that eventful year complete tranquillity seems to have returned until 1924, when a doctor had to be summoned aboard at Shiplake lock to give an emetic to a Billy Bunter who had given himself colic by eating too many plums. And that about sums up the recorded drama of life aboard the steamers.

Had I been walking I should have taken the Abingdon road and passed Bagley Wood, a place I have had a sentimental affection for ever since a girl I knew when I was in my teens gave me Lionel Johnson's poetic ruminations on this very spot, purply stamped on a sheet of pink quarto bank paper with a John Bull printing outfit.

BAGLEY WOOD
by Lionel Johnson

The night is full of stars, full of magnificence:
Nightingales hold the wood, and fragrance loads the dark.
Behold, what fires august, what lights eternal! Hark,
What passionate music poured in passionate love's defence!
Breathe but the wafting wind's nocturnal frankincense!
Only to feel this night's great heart, only to mark
The splendours and the glooms, brings back the patriarch,
Who on Chaldaean wastes found God through reverence.

Could we but live at will upon this perfect height,
Could we but always keep the passion of this peace,
Could we but face unshamed the look of this pure light,
Could we but win earth's heart, and give desire release:
Then were we all divine, and then were ours by right
These stars, these nightingales, these scents: then shame would
    cease.

She had been punting on the Thames with the Lothario whose
place I'd taken, and he'd enticed her ashore and into the wood
and there—presumably after some great catharsis—read to
her this poem which had become as indelibly stamped on
her mind as on the sheet of pink quarto she gave me, perhaps
thinking that I too should entice her into Surrey's equivalent
of Bagley Wood.

I see now that it isn't a very good poem. (Didn't Bernard
Shaw refer to Lionel Johnson as 'a smirking verger'?) But
declaimed in an orotund voice from the slopes of Box Hill—
nothing like Bagley Wood, but higher—I suppose it practically dragged the hearts out of both of us. I can imagine the
mystic meaning I attached to the words 'Chaldaean wastes',
the Raphaelite rosiness that seemed to emanate from us, the
misty distances she would have seen in my cool grey eyes as we
sighed happily and our fingers rumpled the evening dew. (At
seventeen I was a great dew rumpler.)

Good poem or not, it's stayed with me more than thirty
years, along with chunks of *Eskimo Nell* and William Plomer's
The Ballad of Maida Vale, taking up space that should be

stuffed with wodges of *Paradise Lost* and other superior verse,
and I had this tender intention to visit the scene of its inspiration and my first love's romantic fallout. But, instead, I was
aboard this steamer looking out of the neatly curtained saloon
windows at the rain plummeting down on the river. I glimpsed
Bagley Wood across the railway tracks on the starboard side.
No stars, nightingales, or magnificence could be conjured from
the wet scene. I couldn't even evoke the face of the girl or
remember her name. So much for youthful romance. But I
could enjoy the ride, and did.

VI

Pleasure tripping on rivers is a very ancient pastime. Apart
from such royal personages as Cleopatra, whose barge was a
familiar sight on the Nile, and Sennacherib, who was paddled
up and down the Tigris in his galley to enable him to relax
from the strains of re-designing Nineveh, other sorts and conditions of people have at all times since there were boats of any
kind to ride in, enjoyed river trips, with or without objectives.

Until the construction of durable English roads began in
the eighteenth and nineteenth centuries, the Thames, like other
rivers, was of course a highway used mainly for transport. But
this by no means precluded its use as a byway used mainly for
pleasure; and exploitation of that pleasure by those with a
turn for commercial enterprise is as old as the ability to catch
on to a good thing.

To go back no farther than the thirteenth century, for
example, when Eleanor of Provence, the widowed queen of
Henry the Third, wanted to escape from London and her un-
popularity, she made the mistake of thinking that the popularity of her son, the new king Edward the First, would be
her protection. She was mistaken. Londoners particularly were
aware of her continual dipping into Henry's treasury for funds
to support her maternal grandfather, Thomas, who was busily
engaged in trying to resuscitate and expand the House of
Savoy; and they'd had more than enough of Henry's sympathy

'Here, O Father Thames, is your sevenfold fount.' Seven Springs pool

The south entrance to the abandoned Thames–Severn canal

'*History debouches, like the river, on the capital*'

An illustration to a manuscript of poems by
Charles, Duke of Orleans. *c.* 1500

The regatta at Henley, 1891

The fair on the frozen Thames, 1814

An old lock

The old London Bridge

A rough day—Teddington Weir

A fine day—Hampton Court

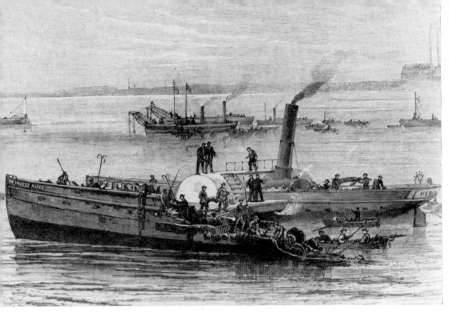

Disaster, 1878—the *Princess Alice*

Disaster, 1928—the floods, Millbank

'An omega-shaped stretch of the Thames'

A view for the tourist

Churchill on his last journey

towards foreigners. Eleanor, a foreigner herself, bore the brunt of their hostility when one of her ladies-in-waiting was bribed —probably by one of Simon de Montfort's henchmen—to reveal the day, time, and manner of the queen dowager's escape.

Since, in these untrustful medieval times, anyone abroad on road or river after dark was suspect, Eleanor's plan was to escape from the Tower of London—in which she was only lightly guarded—in daylight by a small fishing boat in which she could easily pass as a fishwife if suitably clothed. The plan might easily have worked if the bush telegraph had not been set buzzing by the lady-in-waiting's treachery. As it was, residents on London Bridge made a profitable venture of hiring out window space to anyone who wanted to join them in spitting or emptying slops on the queen and her boat as they passed beneath the bridge. But an even shrewder business man, Edwin Sprote, saw that the bridge wouldn't be likely to accommodate all who felt inclined to give Eleanor an ignominious departure; nor would their opportunity be longer than the time necessary for the boat to pass under the bridge. He put word round that he would 'hire to all men at reasonable fee, upon Tamesis so far from Greenwich unto Runnymede, boatmen and their boats in a long line joined that gentil and all men of whatsoever degree that have two pence may convey and make their feast in the meddow and return perhaps the same day and with an chance to mock and pelt the departing queen widdowed of our late King, on whom descrial for her mien unfavoured'. This pleasure trip was a great success. The convoy was of 'six fair boats with canopies' towed by 'two score men with oars in an other'.

Eleanor, having no defences, was duly stoned and spat upon from the bridge and followed all the way by Sprote's convoy, every boat of which was filled to capacity with everyone who'd been able to raise twopence and make the date. These trippers made the most of the day and the most of their chance to mock by bringing with them all the stale eggs and garbage they could find and chucking all with humiliating accuracy at the

H

queen, whose helmsman made numerous attempts to get his boat to the banks and disembark his charge but was always prevented from doing so by other craft on the river or by groups of people who had wedged themselves into the spaces between the houses and were adding their boos and hisses, plus stones and bits of rotting driftwood, to their insulting farewell. Presumably there must have been frequent intervals in which everyone held fire, otherwise Eleanor must surely have been stoned to death; but probably the trippers were filled with scorn rather than hatred and had in any case the edge of their contempt taken off by the novelty of the occasion and the thought of eating their meal at Runnymede and tramping about on the very spot where King John had signed Magna Carta.

Another pleasure trip occasioned by similarly unworthy motives was organised nearly a couple of centuries later, in 1555. 'Fifteen hundred and fifty-five, Ridley and Latimer burnt alive.' I don't know what set the crude mnemonic buzzing in my brain; but it reminded me that on my own innocent journey we were now approaching Abingdon, and that it was from there that some of the ghoulish trippers who watched them burn set out.

Nicholas Ridley and Hugh Latimer were two of the many protestant reformers sent to the stake for heresy by Mary Tudor. Latimer had been strongly favoured by Henry the Eighth because of his approval of the king's wish to divorce Catherine of Aragon. He was often in trouble with the bishops because of his Lutheran opinions, but nonetheless himself became Bishop of Worcester in 1535 and the see remained his until he resigned it after the passing of the Six Articles in 1539 and was imprisoned in the Tower of London until Edward the Sixth succeeded Henry. He was then released and again offered a bishopric; but this time he refused, becoming instead a preacher—largely against the social evils of the day. When Mary, deranged in mind by the syphilis she had inherited from her father, succeeded Edward and began her bloody persecution of protestants, Latimer courageously stayed by his views and refused both to recant and to flee the country—as he could have done. He was sent back to the Tower and from there to Oxford for trial for heresy.

Nicholas Ridley, a much younger man, had similarly reforming opinions, and followed a spectacular career as chaplain to Archbishop Cranmer and later to Henry the Eighth, canon of Canterbury and later of Westminster, Bishop of Rochester and later of London. He then brought about his own downfall by preaching the sermon in which he declared both Mary Tudor (Henry's daughter by Catherine of Aragon) and Elizabeth (his daughter by Anne Boleyn) to be illegitimate and added that the proper heir to the throne was Lady Jane Grey, the protestant great-granddaughter of Henry the Seventh. As soon as Mary Tudor was proclaimed queen he tried to make his peace with her, but, as he might have expected, got no change out of the bloody-minded Mary. He was stripped of all his dignities, sent to the Tower, and in March 1554 was taken from there with Latimer (and Cranmer) to Oxford to await trial.

All three heretics were condemned to death by burning alive, but execution of the sentences was delayed because England was still at loggerheads with Rome. Cranmer accepted the catholic doctrine in his famous recantation and escaped death for the time being, but Ridley and Latimer retracted nothing and after eighteen months in Oxford gaol were brought on 16th October 1555 to the stake that had been set up in front of Balliol College and there set fire to and burnt to death. The Martyrs' Memorial commemorates the execution, and Latimer's cheering allocution to his fellow victim, 'Be of good comfort, Master Ridley, and play the man; we shall this day light such a candle by God's grace in England, as I trust shall never be put out', has gone down in theological history via Foxe's *Book of Martyrs*.

Latimer's metaphor was no mere wry throwaway. The brightness and stench of the candles in the heretical burnings of the Reformation released many emotions. Fear, superstition, religious convictions, symbolism, and the dregs of pagan culture all played a part in the populace's enthusiasm for such spectacles; and it was very easy to stir up interest in people who might otherwise have been indifferent, or put off by the difficulty of getting to the scene of the burning, if you could encourage their inclination to take the line of least resistance and offer them what amounted to a sort of package tour for the occasion. Which is what William and Elizabeth Bates did.

Bates was an educated man who had made a fairish fortune by exhibiting freaks and exotic animals at travelling fairs, and he added to this by organising card games in taverns and blackmailing losing gamblers into working for him and giving them a rakeoff on the money they won for him by becoming proficient cheats under his instruction. He bought a big stone house in Abingdon and from it controlled an underworld gang of cardsharps, brothel touts, and other vicious characters.

Together with his wife Elizabeth, who had acted as a barker in his fairground enterprises, he nosed out any business propositions that might prove profitable. They were skilled in what we should nowadays call 'presentation of the product' —an example of their gimmickry being the corner they made in a cure-all they called 'Salve-ation', which they claimed was an ointment made from a secret recipe and which in an age when puns were the most appealing form of epigrammatic literature worked wonders psychologically—and, of course, commercially—if not therapeutically. The kind of minds that could sort out such a variety of successful commercial ventures were not slow to spot the potentialities of the occasion of the execution of the heretics. Such an event was a spectacle that would bring crowds from distant places—possibly even from London—and Oxford would be full. There would be plenty of opportunities for Bates to sell Salve-ation, to send his emissaries into the taverns with his false dice and marked cards, and to get plenty of business for his brothels. No doubt he seized them. But his most original idea was expressed in a letter to a cousin in Wallingford, to whom he wrote two days before the execution.

'It is ordained and agreed by the burgesses,' he said, 'that the stake do be put up before the college, and that all the burgesses and [those] in authoritie shall orderly go in their best gownes, by two and by two, to witness that the prisoners are properly burned, and dead as is their merit, and a priest to receive their confessions if need be but not put an end to their pain of death in consequence. The prisoners to be garbed in samarras[1] and everyone of the people to be orderly dressed and not drunken before the burning but solemn with no shouting and revels before the flesh scorcheth. After may be an holy day and all may be joy full.

'Which is to say that there will be such business done in the citty that is worthy to take more than ordinary [thought] and I have given it much thought and have decided thus: That it being a temperate season there will be many come from afar, withal from Banbury and farther places and a great concourse will be abroad upon the highways to the North, to the South, to the East, to the West, and I therefore have it in my mind to say to the people here: Assemble here at the wherf all who will at sunrise and I will have a ship for you and you shall travel in it to Oxford and withal save your shoes uppon the highway and on the same time have great merryness aboard her, which I will provide at mine own expense; and there will be food also, and the ship shall return when all is over and the people may take themselves home from here as when they embarked, but with merry hearts for their small expense. I shall put on them a charge of six pennce to the voyage, but on mine own account I shall have in the ship many chances for them to buy pies and ribbons and my oyntment out of the selling [of which] I have done fynely, uppon my oath; and there will be ronfa in plenty, with mine own players, even though I may have to buy the masters faith,[2] should he be

1. A samarra was a loose rough jerkin originally worn by shepherds and later by victims of the Spanish Inquisition.

2. Ronfa was a card game similar to whist and giving card-sharps many opportunies to make tricks with palmed or marked cards; Bates's phrase 'buying the master's faith' probably alludes to the superstition, common among sailors, that cards were 'the Devil's picture books' and were bound to bring ill luck if allowed aboard.

opposed. So they cannot in any manner be scorned of what I shall offer them, for they will also be able to tell those at home of this adventure, which is the first time of doing, as Gods my judge and I know.' (It wasn't, as I've shown; but he may have believed it was.)

The vessel used was probably a barge of some kind with sailing rig. The trippers presumably travelled in the hold which—again presumably—was adapted in the same way for all the activities Bates had planned. These must have been pretty snappily set going, for the journey from Abingdon to Oxford can scarcely have taken more than a couple of hours. But I have no doubt that a man who could run a pleasure trip to a public burning was quite capable of organising everything to his own advantage.

I had thought I might decant myself from my steamer at Abingdon, which was the place I'd originally intended to walk to; but the rain was still soaking down and the thought of it soaking down into the Thames rather than into me was agreeable. Besides, I'd discovered another very good reason for not stopping off at Abingdon: some tourists in the saloon with me. True, there were only three of them, and Abingdon, though not large, is, one would think, large enough to escape from a trio of tourists in. A false premise, the logical truth of it having been knocked cockeyed by my personal exclusion from the laws of probability. These laws work for everyone in the world except me, and naturally I'm delighted to be unique, though I've never swanked about it up to now. But there are snags. One of them is, that if, tired of the skeleton bareness of life, I take myself off to some rich carpet joint and allow myself to be metaphorically maddened by a simple gamble such as tossing a coin with some other wild fool, the laws of probability insist that I have an equal chance with him. But my uniqueness insists otherwise. Similarly, if the laws of probability insist that I am favoured with five hundred chances of being outside the radiations of a noisome trio of bores even within the circumscribed area of a small town like Abingdon, I shall without doubt find myself next to them in the first bar

I go in, or being racked by their commentaries on the top of every bus I board to escape them.

Knowing all this, I make my own special arrangements, which in this case meant deciding to stay on the steamer the tourists planned to get off. How did I know they planned to get off at Abingdon? They were as audible as road-drills and as shatteringly insistent. They were Australians. (I'm just stating a fact, not trying to chip another corner of the Commonwealth off; road-drill bores can be of any nationality.) I will share them with you in a snatch of dialogue (or you can reject your share by turning the page with a sickening thud, which is more than I could).

'Listen, what say we have dinner in Abing*don*?'

'You don't mean dinner, Murray, you mean lunch. How many times . . .'

' "How many times a day do I think of you . . . how many roses are sprinkled with doo . . . how deep is the ocean . . . how far is the journey from here to a star . . ." I forgotten how the words go. You remember how them words go, Melva?'

'Certainly I don't remember it. It was a Crosby, before the war it was. You expect me to remember it at my age?'

'You're a caution, Melva. You know it's a Crosby but you don't remember it. You're a caution. You're a caution, honestly.'

'I know I'm a caution, Angie. An' I know I'm a caution without a Coke. Which of you couple's going to get me a Coke? Anybody want that dinkum honour?'

'I will, Melva. No: let *me*, Murray. I got some change here in my pocket. And tell us what it says in that guide about Abing*don*. I can hear from the bar. These boats are quiet. Aren't these boats quiet, Melva?'

'I'll tell you all right, Angie. Listen to this. "The his-tery of this Birksheer town is an ancient one, for it was famous before its now more famous neighbour across the Thames, Oxford. In Saxon days it was called Ab-ben-doon, the Latin version of which . . ." I'll skip that bit. "Legends of ancient time tell of a British hermit who lived in Abing*don* after a mir-ac-u-lous ecscape from a massacre perp-e-trated by Hengist in the fifth century. But the founding of the town proper was the work of one of the thanes of Wiltshire who granted a site here for the building of a monas-tery. And about the same time (in six-seven-five) a nunnery was founded by the sister of the monk who built the monas-tery. Her name was Cilla and she built the nunnery to house a fragment of one of the nails of the true cross which had been given to her by the Empress Helena. The gift is per-pet-u-ated in the name of the Abing*don* church, St Helen's." You hearing me all right, you sheilas?'

'Loud and clear, Murray boy, you're doin' all right.'

Everybody was hearing him loud and clear. The few centuries following the founding of the nunnery seemed to grind on uncompressed. The details of the sacking of the town by the Danes, the recording in *Domesday Book* of the wealth of the Abingdonians, the rebuilding of the monastery, the looting of the abbey, the pensioning-off of the monks, the erection of the Market House, were read out with all the variation of tone of a defective bagpipe drone.

Then came the riotously funny piece in the guide book explaining that for centuries Abingdon had followed the quaint custom at coronation times of the Mayor and town dignitaries ascending to the roof of the Market House in full fig and throwing buns to the ecstatic populace below. Murray and his sheilas virtually exhausted themselves screaming with laughter at this revelation of English drollery. But there was still stronger stuff to come. The compiler of the guide book had also noted that the buns were often preserved as trophies by the lucky citizens grabbing them—varnished, labelled, and displayed in glass cases; and he had waggishly commented: 'I daresay they become, more or less, rock cakes!' The subtlety of this sally touched the very nub of the trio's comic sense. 'They fell about with laughter' is a phrase often used to describe an audience's reaction. I have always accepted it as a bit of Public Relations guff. But I can use it with accuracy in this case. All three of them were seized with fits of raucous shrieks that clearly were going to rock them through many a captive audience in the future. I felt tiny stigmata on my heart for the unwitting listeners who might silt up with them. And each time eyes were wiped, sips at glasses taken, and hands removed from aching sides some new quaintness in the guide book would catch the eye of one of them.

'You see this, Murray, Angie?—"Camden described it as a 'very famous city goodly to behold, full of riches, encompassed about with very fruitful fields, with green meadows, spacious pastures, and flocks of cattle abounding with milk' " —ho, ho, ho—"*en-com-passed about*!" O God I shall die, I know I shall die——!'

'And here's a bit by Peep-is, lookie, in his diary where he says "At night came to Abingdon, where had been a fair of *custard*". Can you beat that—*custard* . . . !'

More excruciating ho-ho-hos. And even a quotation from Defoe stating the plain fact 'they make great quantities of malt here, and send it by barges up to London' couldn't diminish their enthusiasm for the drolleries of English humour. I was fascinated in a deadly way, but not quite enough to believe I wouldn't get a better deal from the rain.

As it happened, I did. There was a small neat man with glasses and a pointed beard who had come on deck for the same escapist reason, and after nodding in gloomy sympathy to each other we stood tentatively testing each other's reactions to further conversation. For people who have just escaped, scathed and sore, from the kind of setup I have shown you the fringe of ('fringe' is right; there were inner convolutions I haven't ventured to show) there are serious uses for the antennae of sensitivity. One daren't risk further bruising, but the restorative balm of a few quiet conversational words is worth seeking. One tests, very carefully.

'Rain's refreshing?'

'Refreshing indeed.'

Two minutes used for assessment. So far all seems safe.

'Soothing.'

'I feel so.'

This is tantamount to acceptance, which is acknowledged by another two minutes' interval, this time just to explore parallel silences on the same wavelength. A satisfying exploration. In it one may feel grateful for the occasional juxtaposition of kindred spirits, neatly arranged by fate to compensate for the much more frequent juxtaposition of non-kindred ones.

My bearded companion entertained me with an anecdote and a sliver of history—both of which I can justifiably jockey into position here since both had this stretch of the Thames as a setting.

The anecdote was about an Oxford don who, strolling through Christ Church Meadow one Sunday morning encountered one of his students strolling in the opposite direction.

'And why, sir,' he asked the student, 'are you not in chapel?'

'Because I don't believe in God, sir.'

'In that case, sir, you will form a belief in God by three o'clock this afternoon. Otherwise you will leave the college.'

A nice example of instant conversion.

The bit of history concerned Nuneham Park, which we had been steaming past for some time at reduced speed—'so that passengers may have a chance of observing in leisurely manner the beauties of the overhanging woods, the mansion with the "Capability" Brown gardens, and the historic Lock Cottage and its linking rustic bridge', the trip handout explained.

Taking off his glasses to wipe the rain from them and settling them carefully away in their case, my companion enlightened me about the park.

'It belongs to the university now—they bought it in nineteen-forty-seven. Before that just two families stretched their ownership of the place over seven hundred years. First there were the Courtenays, who settled in there in the twelve-hundreds. One of them, William—I forget his dates, but he was fourteenth century anyway—was chancellor of the uni-

versity and later Bishop of Hereford, then London, then Archbishop of Canterbury. He was the one who opposed Wycliffe
and the Lollards. The Courtenays were there till seventeen-
ten, then the Harcourts bought it from them and moved in.

'The Harcourts had a lineage as long and noble as the
Courtenays', and they'd always lived on the Thames too, but
up river a bit, at Stanton Harcourt. Simon Harcourt, who
bought Nuneham from the Courtenays, was Lord Chancellor
at the time, and he had a grandson who was Lord-high-every-
thing else. A despot if ever there was one. The village was by
the river then, a straggly place that had just evolved over the
years, cottages the people had put up themselves because they
liked the place—and, as you see, it's pretty enough. But this
wouldn't do for Harcourt. The house, which was built for
him by a chap named Leadbetter, who built the Radcliffe
Infirmary in Oxford and Foley House in London, had a
marvellous view down to the river—except that the village
got in the way. That was enough for Harcourt. He simply
commanded the villagers to knock down their own cottages
and rebuild them along the north edge of the wood, where
they wouldn't interfere with his view and anyway were outside the walls of his park—"beyond the pale", as they say. I've
always cherished that nice little example of feudalism.'

I cherished it too, and set down the details on the back of
the handout. As we were at the moment passing the island
that was linked to the park by the rustic bridge referred to as
'historic' I asked my companion if he knew what was historic
about it.

'Nothing specially that I know of,' he said. 'Boats used to
pass round the other side of the island, and underneath the
bridge, where there was a flash-lock—you know, the old kind
that simply tumbled the boat down the slope and left it to
pick itself up at the bottom. But I don't think it's been used
for nearly a couple of centuries. It was much easier for everything to sail round this side of the island and avoid the bump
altogether. I think that's about the only history it has. But it
gets photographed a lot'—he nudged me—'as you see.'

I turned and found that despite the rain most of our fellow trippers—including the road-drills—had emerged on deck and were getting cameras posed and exposure meters turned towards the uniformly grim sky. We paced to the starboard side, concentrated on the Berkshire bank, and made our concentration last until the view was safely locked away in Leicas and Rolleiflexes and everyone had returned to the saloon.

'Unfortunately,' he continued, tilting his head forward so that a small cascade of rainwater fell from the brim of his hat, 'I have to get off at Abingdon, where I'm expected for lunch. I hope our Commonwealth friends don't choose the same place as my host to lunch in.'

I told him that it was to avoid the possibility of a similar encounter that I had decided to go on as far as Reading. We said our rainswept and sympathetic farewells at Abingdon lock and I returned to the saloon to find Murray, Melva, and Angie still shrieking their way raucously through the guide book and being told by a glassy-eyed steward that if they wanted to see Abingdon they'd better start now, Sir, Madam, 'because this is where you get off if you still want to make it'.

They gathered up their traps with cries of astonishment, and, I'm happy to say, made it.

6

Pollution and Bogglesloshing

I

QUEEN VICTORIA spent part of her honeymoon at
Nuneham Park. Her standard flew from the central block of
Harcourt's Palladian mansion, precisely above the royal bed-
room in the middle, and in several letters she referred to the
view across the valley and down the river as 'very fine' and
'remarkably fine', which it doubtless was and is, though I
couldn't sample it myself. But her diary and voluminous correspondence show that her interests were by no means limited
to landscapes and marriage. Nor were those of her husband,
Prince Albert. Albert had many acquaintances in the field
of science, and presumably from them he gained the geological knowledge that he passed on to the queen during their
honeymoon tête-à-têtes. One would have thought geology to be
rather heavy going as a subject for honeymoon conversation,
but the queen evidently took it in her stride. She wrote to
one of her ladies-in-waiting, a daughter of the Earl of
Southampton :

'. . . I recall [Albert] giving me some interesting intelligence, when we were at Nuneham Park, that for me threw
new light on the River Thames. At the old Roman towns of
Goring and Streatley the river turns its course from the Moulsford Downs through the Chiltern Hills. But it was not always
so. In prehistoric times, before the Hills were formed as the
earth cooled down, the river made its course to the north from
Moulsford and from there to join the Great Ouse and eventu-

ally to find its way into the Wash. Is not this something we should think of as exemplifying the constant changes of nature?'

The changes of nature may be constant, but the geological ones are very slow, and it took several million years for the midland river system to wear its devious ways through the hills and for the Thames to find a new channel when its course to the Wash became barred by the great ice formations of the Pleistocene era. But find one it did through the chalk of the Chilterns, and flowed on to join the Kennet at Reading instead of the Wash on the east coast—or, earlier, the Rhine in the middle of what eventually became the North Sea.

However long it took for the Thames to chisel its way through Goring Gap, the time was well spent if you judge the result by the beauty of its course. I am not given to idyllic descriptive passages—my own sicken me and other writers' invariably seem inadequate—but I will say that I found the journey through the Gap enchanting even in pouring rain. There is this to be said about leisurely steamer travel—it allows plenty of time to enjoy the view. Much of it is of course accounted for by the time one spends in locks. There are forty-seven of them on the Thames and they follow each other in rapid succession all the way down to Teddington. The longest un-locked stretch is between Benson, just west of Wallingford, and Cleeve, just west of Goring; and that's no more than six-and-a-half miles. Until relatively recently it was even shorter, for there were a couple more locks at Wallingford and Moulsford, both in the Benson–Cleeve stretch. They were both flash locks and both were demolished in 1793. The Wallingford one was replaced by a pound lock in 1838, but that too was done away with in 1883 after bitter discussions in the press and at public meetings, thousand-signature petitions to the Thames Conservators, and in general a hoo-hah of such magnitude that even New York heard about it in a lecture given by an alderman of Wallingford who had been invited to talk on 'English Home Economy in these days of the Queen Empress'.

An ugly scene threatened when workmen came to demolish the lock and an irate bargee in a small crowd of bystanders chucked a half brick and the foreman of the workers chucked it back. Only the presence of mind of the bargee's wife, who gained an appreciative shout from the crowd by fielding the brick, saved the situation. But letters in the press and other demonstrations of disapproval of the highhanded action of the Conservators continued for some time. As late as 1885 snide remarks were being made about 'Conservators who conserve nothing but the water round their brains', and the comic magazine *Fun* rattled on for several issues about the dangers of impeding river traffic by the abolition of locks when the railways had already 'robbed our river and canal systems of most of their commerce'. This was prejudiced exaggeration. The railways had certainly taken most of the inland waterways transportation; but there could never have been any impeding of traffic by the removal of a lock that was in any case 'a summer or low water lock' with both its gates fixed open throughout the time when the volume of water was taken care of by the average English rainfall—which meant virtually always.

While we were in the lock at Goring and Streatley the rain eased off. I decided to leave the steamer there and board the next one, due down at ten o'clock the following morning. I felt inclined to walk the three miles or so along the Oxfordshire bank of the river as far as Pangbourne, cross there, and return to Streatley—which sits opposite Goring across the river—and stay the night at the Swan Hotel.

It was nearly four o'clock when I disembarked and I started my diversionary tour by sampling Goring's spring water in place of afternoon tea. I had come across a reference to this in the 1794 file of my local paper—perhaps I should say a eulogy rather than a reference, for there were some three hundred names under a statement praising its curative qualities—and I wanted to sample it. True, I hadn't any of the maladies it was famous for curing—scurvy, skin ulcers, and rhinophyma—but I had a thirst. The water was tasteless, like the Malvern spring water that is sold as an additive to whisky; but this in itself is something, for most water nowadays is necessarily so 'purified' with chemicals that it is often actively unpleasant. Apart from this I didn't notice myself feeling any better after it. However, I summoned up enough strength to begin to walk.

With characteristic inability to take the right turning if there are two or more to choose from, I turned the wrong way in Goring village and walked nearly a mile before I thought I recognised a familiar scene and found myself back at Cleeve lock, which the steamer had gone through very shortly before reaching Goring. I was in no way surprised. (During the war I managed to lead my troop of tanks into a field from which there was no escape except into the face of the enemy, and no-one was very pleased about that, since our business at the time was retreat, not battle. However, as you know, we won the war in spite of my efforts.) I was rather pleased that I cleverly recognised the scene I had passed all of an hour ago and thereby saved myself from walking farther in the wrong direction.

It would in any case have been inconvenient to continue along this road, even if I'd wanted to go that way, because it was deeply flooded with the morning's heavy rain. The road formed a long step cut into the hillside and its camber turned it into an efficient trough to impede and contain the storm water as it ran off this outcrop of the Chilterns. There wasn't very much traffic, but what there was was sending up great gushes of flood water as it sped along. Certainly all the motorists coming from Goring could see well ahead and knew exactly what was happening to the cars in front of them; but they seemed fascinated by the great swathes of water their vehicles could send up if driven fast, and they drove them at unremitting speed. They reminded me of children who can't resist jumping into a puddle when they've got their best shoes and socks on but will resist one all day if suitably shod for puddle jumping. However, what mainly occupied my thoughts as I retraced my steps and continued my way through Goring and on to the road going east, was the whole business of the conservation of water.

II

Unlike many tropical countries, Britain has never had a serious general problem of water supply. Except in occasional droughty years our normal rainfall takes care of that. But local problems arise with the gradual concentration of population in particular areas, and these problems have had to be tackled. The methods of tackling them are not without interest.

Any area into which water drains naturally—as by running from the higher to the lower levels of hills into rivers, lakes, or ponds—or is conducted artificially—as by pump and pipe into man-made reservoirs—is called a catchment area. A land such as England is riddled with underground springs and wells, and when these have been fortuitously detached they have naturally attracted the settlement of people nearby. In the earliest times everyone simply went with a container to the well or point where digging had revealed a spring and collected the water; later, people realised that it would save trouble if they built their houses below the level of the nearest water supply and ran the water along miniature aqueducts of tiles, or through wood or metal pipes to a convenient point such as a village pump or a storage tank. Such tanks, or cisterns, are in effect private catchments, and there are a great number of them still in use in rural Britain today. However, on the principle of the greatest good of the greatest number, municipal water supplies have gradually developed and legal and administrative difficulties of immense complexity have developed with them. Not understanding these, I shall only make a bow in their direction and then ignore them. My business is with the Thames as a catchment area.

I

In England before Magna Carta rivers belonged, like many other things, to the king—anyway in theory. He had power to do much as he liked with them, including the power to grant specified people the exclusive right to fish in them and take the water for personal use, and to restrict or prohibit navigation upon them wherever and whenever he thought fit. Exercised in excess this power defeated its own ends, for rivers are natural channels of communication and the king's private purse suffered with the national economy if commerce was restricted by nit-witted exclusion laws. Magna Carta straightened out this anomalous position by defining the tidal stretches of rivers with outlets to the sea as being public property, the ownership being vested in the crown on behalf of the people. The non-tidal bits, and all inland rivers, remained privately owned by the people through whose land they ran; but as channels of communication they gradually acquired some navigation rights by custom ('immemorial use' is the legal phrase) and had others thrust upon them by Act of Parliament.

In the pre-Magna Carta days the king could also command the exclusive use of rivers to slake his thirst—and indeed he quite often did when part of a river ran in or near his garden. But clearly his power couldn't be usefully applied in the case of large catchment areas such as those of the Thames (simply guarding such an area would have presented insuperable practical problems) and the provisions of Magna Carta merely fixed as law the public ownership that was already established by custom.

Ownership of a river by the people as a whole implies planned protection, or conservation, against several things—among them excessive demands on the available quantity of water, pollution, unfair monopoly of the navigable parts of the river by too large or too numerous craft, indiscriminate fishing that might bring some kinds of fish to extinction, and storage of water to meet the demands of the increasing population. Such conservation is administratively complex, and the king must often have found it irksome to look after the tidal rivers for which he had been made responsible on behalf of his people. Watermen and engineers in abundance were needed and they all had to be paid. Their pay would in the final analysis come from the people by way of taxes, naturally; but many a king could find better use for taxes than that.

Henry the Seventh was the one that shifted the burden so far as the Thames was concerned. In 1487 he gave the river —water, bed, and foreshore up to the high water mark of its tidal part—into the charge of the Lord Mayor and people of London. The gift was rather snootily referred to as 'The granting of the conservancy of our royal Tamesis from henceforth for all time . . .', as if London had been for years entreating the king to let them look after their river. But this grandiloquence didn't conceal the fact that he was glad to be rid of his responsibility. Successive Lord Mayors and their corporations coped according to their abilities, well or ill, with their new responsibility until 1857, when twelve conservators were appointed and the Thames Conservancy Board officially came into being.

Half a century later, in 1908, the Conservancy's responsibility was limited to the non-tidal part of the river (that is, above Teddington) and the Port of London Authority took control of the rest of it down to the Nore. A number of amendments were made to the Acts that divided the responsibilities and by 1932 complexity had become muddle and the entire setup of Acts was repealed and a consolidating Thames Conservancy Act replaced them. Since the work of conservation was itself continually becoming more complex the 1932 Act was again amended in 1950, and it then gave the conservators power to increase both their revenue and their number, and there are now thirty-eight—their executive officers being a Chairman, Vice-Chairman, Secretary, Treasurer, and Chief Engineer—whose duty calls them to conserve the river above Teddington. Their watchful eye must consider pollution of the main stream and its tributaries, keep its docks and canals in good repair, protect its fisheries, control its navigation, and see that the land drainage of the entire catchment area is working properly. This, as you may imagine, is no sinecure.

True, there are no docks above Teddington and most of the canals, like the Thames-Severn, have long fallen into disuse and are content to hide themselves under an overgrowth of weeds; but two thousand three hundred and eighty-two miles of main and tributary river offer plenty of scope for attention. For niceness of judgement too. There is still a flow of contentious letters between the conservators and some riverside residents who like to think that the rights of immemorial use can be ignored and that they are still bosses of the river itself as well as the banks it flows between.

For example, at Mapledurham Mill on the Oxford-shire bank of the river four miles west of Reading, the main channel passes on the starboard side of an island and a picturesque backwater flows round the port side. This is a great attraction for people in small boats who fancy photographing the Mill itself. They get short shrift from the land-owner's guardians, who bellow at them to clear off because this is private water. As I've explained, there isn't any private water on the Thames so far as navigation of vessels is concerned, and hasn't been for hundreds of years; but you have only to tell the ordinary Englishman that he's invading someone's privacy and he scuttles off full of contrition. It's only when you get one who's dubious about the sacredness of archaic laws that an appeal is made to the conservators. But it happens often enough for the conservators to keep in draft a formal letter in which they sharply rap landowners over the knuckles for attempting to prevent the free passage of vessels along any part of the river.

However, though niceness of judgement is indispensable in dealing with such ticklish legal matters, it is with the much weightier affairs I've listed that the conservators are chiefly concerned. Pollution, for instance. And here it is continual vigilance that is indispensable.

Without going into incomprehensible flights of chemical analysis I will explain what pollution means in respect to the Thames.

Broadly, clean river water is pure to the extent of being

drinkable without harmful effects because it contains oxygen. The oxygen is absorbed from the air and dissolved in the water, and so long as there is one pound of oxygen in every ten thousand gallons of water the river remains clean. Rivers of course support their own animal and vegetable life by the oxygen in them; but if more organic matter is added this will become oxidised through the agency of bacteria and the oxygen content of the water will be correspondingly depleted. The amount of depletion will naturally be in proportion to the amount of organic matter added.

If, for example, a dead cat is thrown into a clean river the decomposition of the carcase is an organic change that will use up some of the oxygen, but not enough to make any measurable difference, because the water is continually flowing from upstream of the carcase and bearing fresh supplies of oxygen—far more than is needed to accomplish the decomposition. But if the excretions of a million people are collected and thrown into the same spot there will be an immediate depletion of the oxygen below the one-pound-in-ten-thousand-gallons level, because this too is organic matter that will go through a chemical change via the agency of bacteria, using up oxygen in the process. The river will remain impure on the downstream side of the deposited excretions until time and its surface area have restored the balance by the absorption of sufficient new oxygen. If you continue to put excretions in the water in the form of town sewage, and also continue to increase the quantity, there will eventually come a point at which the oxidation of organic matter in the water is using up more oxygen than the river can absorb from the air. The river will then become poisonous and nauseating, giving off a horrid stench, which is hydrogen sulphide, and a miasma that bites into lead paint and turns all the brasswork in the neighbourhood completely black. Clearly, such a state is most likely to prevail at the tidal end of the river, because there the incoming tides will counteract the tendency of the outgoing ones to wash the effluential content out to sea.

In a modern society it is of course not only human sewage that is conducted into rivers. Street drains discharging into them carry off rainwater from the gutters and with it a good deal of mud and muck; the collected garbage of whole cities is deposited in them; electricity generating stations draw water from them for use in cooling systems and return it in heated form, which means that the oxygen content is further depleted; the reduction of atmospheric pollution from the same power stations by washing the flue gases results in an increase in the pollution of rivers because the washing water returned to them contains sulphite which again reduces the oxygen; and the waste products of innumerable industries, from coal gas to nuclear physics, are all piped riverwards.

Although all this contamination goes on to a considerable extent in the upper part of the Thames—much of it coming from the larger towns like Oxford and Reading—it is naturally the tidal portion that suffers most—not only because of its tidal nature but also because of the enormous outfalls of sewage and the rest of the mess from London and its sprawling suburbs. It is possible to treat both sewage and industrial effluents and reduce the amount of organic matter in them (this is done by sedimentation, filtration, and aeration); but enough oxidisable organic matter remains to give the Port of London Authority a continual headache, in both figurative and literal senses; and I shall give a rundown on the extensive investigations the PLA has made in its attempts to cope, when I come to the area of its control.

The Thames Conservancy has in comparison a negligible pollution problem. At the foot of Teddington weir, where its responsibility ends, the river is invariably completely saturated with dissolved oxygen, and it also contains healthy proportions of nitrate which has the effect of increasing still further the supplies of oxygen. So you might say that the TC passes over to its opposite number, the PLA, a river in the best possible condition. But it has other problems, notably to ensure that not only the quality of the water, but also the quantity, is high enough. To enlighten you on the size of this problem I

will quote from a government departmental report put out by
a committee in 1961. (This committee was investigating the
pollution of the tidal Thames, but its investigations naturally
included statistics on the input of water at the beginning of
the tidal reach.)

'The flow of the Upper Thames has been gauged at Teddington Weir by the Thames Conservancy ever since 1883, when
they undertook this task at the suggestion of the Royal Commission on Metropolitan Sewage Discharge. The maximum
amount recorded, which occurred in the floods of November
1894, was over twenty thousand million gallons a day; the
lowest—seventeen million gallons a day—was in October
1934.

'Natural variations in rainfall and runoff are the main
reason for the wide range of flows encountered, but at the
lower end of the scale the abstraction of water by the Metropolitan Water Board for public supply makes a material
difference. Over the year the Board's intakes from Staines to
Teddington provide them with an average of about two
hundred and thirty m.g.d., or a little more than two-thirds of
their present requirements. Most of this water is eventually
returned to the tidal waters of the Thames as sewage effluent.
The Board vary their rates of abstraction according to need,
their practice being to fill up their reservoirs as fast as possible
when there is plenty of flow in the river. The quantity they
take is subject to statutory restrictions: the permitted maximum is twelve hundred m.g.d., but the most they have ever
abstracted in one day is four hundred and fifty-six m.g.d. Of
more importance, in practice, is the permitted average of abstraction of three hundred m.g.d. in a calendar year. . . .

'These abstraction powers are subject to the condition that
a mimimum of a hundred and seventy m.g.d.—"the statutory
minimum"—must be left flowing over Teddington Weir.'

To ensure that those daily millions of gallons are available
to be drawn off by the Metropolitan Water Board for the
benefit of London's thirsty millions and still leave at least a
hundred and seventy million gallons toppling over the weir

would of course be relatively simple, except in times of drought, if there were not a steadily increasing number of further thirsty millions to be taken care of in the Conservancy's own area of the Upper Thames. But as things are there is a continual pressing need to draw off adequate supplies for storage when the river's flow is high and to find new independent supplies. Both these activities demand big expenditure for reservoirs and experimental boreholes. And for this, of course, there is never enough money. Many towns in the Thames Valley can drain off supplies from tributary rivers, but this can only have the ultimate effect of diminishing the flow of the Thames. Reading, for example, takes a goodly proportion of its water from the Kennet; but to leave the tributary flow adequate, supplementary supplies are drawn from boreholes and deep wells at Pangbourne.

However they look at it, the conservators are faced with a watery version of the law of diminishing returns. Their plight must seem to them most irksome during times such as that into which I fitted my excursion to Pangbourne. The river was running fairly high after all the rain and I could imagine them banging frustrated heads against walls of economic resistance that prevented them building more reservoirs to trap water that was rapidly flowing away but which someone would be screaming for sooner or later. However, as I said some pages back, Britain can at least forget about the problem of water supply, if not about the problem of storage.

III

Perhaps it was as well that my plans were as fluid as the river, for at Pangbourne I chanced to meet a man who'd been in the army with me—had, in fact, been operating the wireless in the very tank in which I'd led the regiment to its unscheduled battle (not that I reminded him of that). He was called Lofty for one of the customary witless reasons that seem to govern army nomenclature: he was short. I remembered him as a cheerful soul with a built-in mania for motor-cars and the turn of humour that's often thought of as whimsical, though not by me; and both these characteristics, I saw at once, were unchanged. They were exemplified in tandem in the car he was driving—a Clyno saloon of about 1928. Its fabric-covered body was in immaculate condition, its thick-spoked wheels had been painted bright yellow, two chromium bars in front of the radiator carried eight assorted fog and spot lamps and the insignia of a dozen motoring organisations, there were two radio antennae and a couple more fog lamps flanking the windscreen, and the spare wheel below the rear window was shrouded in an oilskin cover on which was written 'Madam, don't laugh—your daughter may be inside'. A riot of ebullience, as you see.

Lofty recognised me while I was passing the Nautical College—a rather grand name for an anchored sailing ship in which young men are trained for the navy. Some obstruction ahead had stopped the Oxford-bound traffic and the Clyno had pulled up beside me. His cries of astonishment had heads popping from windows right down the line of cars. Hand pumping and the trotting out of phrases usual on these occasions took a minute or two, and by that time there was movement ahead. Since I was going in the same direction I couldn't gracefully have refused a lift, and anyway I wasn't sure that I wanted to. A three-mile walk combined with meditation on the functions of the Thames Conservancy is exhausting for a man of my age.

Lofty said he was 'whizzing down to Nuneham to give the old flivver her daily dozen before I show her off in the Cranky Cars Rally at Reading'. Clearly the pleasure he took in being thought a wag was great. Every time another motorist, or a pedestrian, looked at the car and steadily absorbed the great joke, Lofty beamed with satisfaction. He fed out of the window jolly little conversation-pieces like 'Any more for the Skylark?' and 'There's no Tiger in my tank—just a gentle pussy' and the onlooker who responded with a laugh or a thumbs-up sign was accepted as being deep in the rib-tickling business with him. Bonhomie was their call-sign and the world would never have a dull moment if they had their way. No rib-tickler myself, I found it salutary to be at the winnowing end of this harvest of corn. I had no comparable offering to make to the world. But if I deny you the comedy of the ride it is only so that I can keep to my own script and concentrate on the river. The lift in Lofty's Cranky Car in fact enabled me more conveniently to look at one or two places I'd drifted by in the steamer and had decided I must return to.

Sutton Courtenay and Culham, for instance, which face each other across the river just below Abingdon. They are both picturesque in the traditional English way, and about that fact I shall remain wordless. I shall allow the English politician Herbert Henry Asquith to speak instead. He said many things beside 'wait and see', and one of them was about Sutton Courtenay, where he made his home. He wrote to his son, 'Its charm, peace, and beauty are to me the real essence of England.' His house 'The Wharf' backs on to three weirs that mark the division of the river into two courses—a division he commented on in one of his orotund parliamentary speeches as 'symbolic of the split in the Liberal Party'. Which, as things turned out, was a symbol that didn't sustain its symbolism, for, at the end of Culham Cut, the river joins itself together again, but the Liberals never managed to do that.

But politicians have often found the Thames useful for anal-ogies—perhaps because they have so many opportunities of observing it as it flows past the Houses of Parliament. I've already mentioned John Burns and his comment about the Thames being 'liquid 'istory'. Another one, Ned Evans, who spent a great deal of his parliamentary career crusading for the old and deaf, once remarked to me that if by his efforts he could unmuffle the sounds of London's river for all the people who lived within normal earshot but were precluded by disability from hearing them, he would have accomplished as great a triumph as Pasteur. And Winston Churchill—also a Liberal in his time—said of Asquith's later parliamentary speeches that they were 'like the river that runs beside his home

—muddy and unpredictable'. This in itself is statesman's wind-blown rhetoric, for the Thames throughout its length is never truly unpredictable in its behaviour, and at Sutton Courtenay it certainly isn't muddy. However, analogies are illustrative rather than definitive.

Steamers follow the route through Culham Cut to avoid the weirs at the bottom of the late Mr Asquith's garden, and as my map of the river had a note saying 'After passing through the lock it is well worth while to turn back up the weir stream and backwaters which run up to Sutton Courtenay for they are generally considered the most beautiful on the Thames', I asked Lofty to pause on our return journey and let me take in, from a better vantage point, the idyllic beauty so often rapturously described. The island between the cut and the main stream was buzzing with photographers trying to get new angles on this bit of scenery. There was also a lady composing verses for birthday cards, and she told me she could find inspiration for these poetic gems only here and at Mortlake 'where the boat race ends'. Since Mortlake's river frontage is taken up mainly by a large ugly brewery I asked her if the Mortlake-inspired part of her output tended to be stark and the Sutton Courteney part bowery. But she said no, she found Mortlake inspiring chiefly because Oliver Cromwell was born there.

She was wrong there. Oliver was born miles away in Huntingdon. I said, 'I think you mean Thomas, don't you?' She wanted to know who Thomas was and I told her he was Oliver's ancestral uncle and was born not at Mortlake but at Putney. 'Oh well,' she said. 'That's near enough.' I left the lady to brood over her *non sequiturs*, her garbled history, and her verses; but she had at least reminded me that both Thomas and Oliver had associations with the Thames that are worth noting.

Thomas's father kept a pub adjoining a forge beside the towpath at Putney, and from there, in 1504, Thomas set out at the age of nineteen to make money. He had as capital the then equivalent of £2, which he very probably stole from the pub till, and he used this to buy from Thames fishermen salmon which he later sold to the commissariat at Windsor Castle, bypassing the official provisioners to the advantage of both himself and the royal cooks by doubling the normal prices and splitting the difference with them. He then took ship and sailed down the river to make an even bigger fortune than the £100 net profit he accumulated from his provisioning. This time he went as far as France and Italy, teamed up with the Florentine banker Frescobaldi, and became a lawyer and moneylender.

In 1513 he returned to England 'clad by day and night in the finest of silkes and furres' and married the girl next door, Elizabeth Wykes, an ancestor of mine. Cardinal Wolsey turned him into a tax collector and from then onward he travelled a long, if twisted, road to power and fortune. He became in succession a privy councillor to Henry the Eighth, chancellor of the exchequer, master of the rolls, vicar general, knight of the Garter, Dean of Wells, and Earl of Essex. He was, as Hilaire Belloc says, Henry's 'chief instrument in the suppression of the monasteries. His lack of all fixed principle, his unusual power of application to a particular task, his devotion to whatever orders he chose to obey, and his quite egregious avarice, all fitted him for the work his master ordered. How the witty scoundrel accomplished that business is a matter of common history. Had he never existed the monasteries would have fallen just the same, perhaps in the same manner, and probably with the same despatch. But fate has chosen to associate this revolution with his name—and to his presence in that piece of confiscation we owe the presence in history of the great Oliver; for Oliver . . . and all his tribe were fed upon no other food than the possessions of the Church.'

As you may imagine, Cromwell was the most hated of the Reformers, and because he had climbed so high to power he had a long way to fall when his turn came. It came as a result of Henry's marriage to Anne of Cleves, which he arranged and which, as everyone knows, Henry was far from pleased with. The morning after the bridal night Henry said to Cromwell: 'I liked her not well before, and now I like her much worse. She has ill smells about her. I have touched her belly and her breasts and, as I judge, she is no virgin.' Henry's tetchiness with the Flanders Mare was much boosted by Cromwell's enemies, who caused him to be arrested and and charged with heresy and high treason and flung into the Tower of London. From there he sent to the king a plea for mercy, 'the which failing,' he added with some dignity, 'I crave of your highnesse that my body should find its grave in the river that I know to be my birthright (for was I not born beside it?) and would welcome as my right in death allso, if your highnesse faileth me not in your sometime love'.

After some hesitation on the part of the king, who needed Cromwell's evidence to ease his divorce from Anne and shrewdly saw that he could raise the prisoner's hopes of release by letting him think he might be swapping the evidence for his freedom, Cromwell's head was chopped off on Tower Hill on 28th July 1540. His executioner remarked to the jailer that 'his body doth incarnadine Tamesis to a sanguine beauty uncommon in the mud hereabouts'.

Oliver's association with the Thames in the instance I have in mind was also bloody; but on this occasion it was the blood of war that was spilt into the river—as so often before, but now for the last time.

The first Civil War ended in the summer of 1646. The besieging of Wallingford, one of the few remaining garrisons held by the Royalists, went on for sixteen weeks, and when at last it fell Oliver Cromwell ordered the immediate annihilation of the king's soldiers who had so staunchly defended the castle. Cromwell witnessed the execution by decapitation and ordered that both heads and bodies be flung into the river. 'Enough of the stench of war,' he said to his general, Fairfax, 'and enough of the stench of rottenness too. Let the river have them before they corrupt the land as the king corrupted England.'

I mentioned this to Lofty as we were driving over Wallingford Bridge—from which Cromwell, seated on his horse, watched the executions. He said 'Oh' without much interest and told me he was driving back via North Stoke, where there was some wild watercress he wanted to pick for his supper sandwiches. ('The wilder the better, eh?—and I'll be wild if I don't find some.') There was indeed wild watercress, in a small mill pond fed from the river; but I was more interested in finding Brook Lodge, the home of a once famous contralto, Clara Butt. She was the singer for whom Elgar wrote his *Sea Pictures*; but the tastes of her times were for ballads of nauseating sentimentality in the words and excruciating chromaticism in the music, and it was her records of these that sold in thousands. I once possessed a couple of them—a repellent bit of geriatric twaddle called *In the Chimney Corner* and *Abide With Me* fitted to a tune drenched in vulgarity.

I remember mentioning Miss Butt and her fortune-making records to a friend of mine, Joe Batten, who was a king pin in the artists' booking department of the company that sponsored her. He told me that she was successful with this tenth-rate music because she had in her the particular kind of interpretive sensitivity a singer needs to counteract its abysmal triviality. Consequently, she could put such songs over as if they were of real worth.

Then he added that he'd been down to Brook Lodge on a business visit one day and been told by her husband, Kennerley Rumford, that she was down by the river 'drawing inspiration from it'. Batten, who'd spent his working life being tactful with performing artists, had no trouble in keeping straight-faced even though the picture conjured up was a risible one; but when he went through the garden in search of her he found it to be not far off a depiction of the literal truth. She had arranged herself, with an eye to carefully studied composition, in a reclining posture on the bank and was holding to her ear a large conch shell into which she had scooped a gill of Thames water. 'I have to sing a new song about a babbling brook,' she said, 'and I am listening to the sound of babbling.'

It pleased me to look at a bit of the river that had fulfilled such an odd purpose. It was like finding the ballet school where Mr Beverley Nichols's daffodils had learnt to dance. I got aboard the Clyno as satisfied as was Lofty with his haul of wild watercress, and we drove on eastward down the road towards Goring. Much of the flood water I had seen during my walk along it in the afternoon had drained off, but Frampton cut speed to a crawl, not wanting to get his showpiece muddied up. It was dark now and he could no longer rely on being the star of the road. This had the effect of making long gaps in his bonhomie and into these, with more or less kindly intentions, I fed scraps of guide-book material. ('We are now passing South Stoke, where stands the church in which Cromwell stabled his cavalry during the siege of Wallingford; across the river is the ancient hostelry known as The Beetle and Wedge, and a mile upstream is Cholsey with the remains of the tenth-century monastery founded by Ethelred the Unready in atonement for the murder of Edward the Martyr by his stepmother, Elfrida.') But this seemed to depress him even more. However, I chattered remorselessly on about Kenneth Grahame, who lived in Pangbourne (though he didn't write *The Wind in the Willows* there), and Thomas Morton, who not only lived there but also, in 1798, invented Mrs Grundy there.[1] Lofty cheered up a bit, though, when I mentioned Bogglesloshing. This is Pangbourne's modern version of the old custom of making sacrificial offerings to the Thames river god King Lud. It involves the stripping to the Y-fronts of a young man (chosen by lot) who is subsequently daubed with paint, hurled into the river, prevented by other lusty young men from landing until the limit of his endurance has been reached, and finally hosed down with a stirrup pump while the onlookers jeer at his discomfiture.

1. She was invented in a bucolic play called *Speed the Plough*. The dialogue in which she is simultaneously created and accoladed with immortality is as follows: 'Be quiet wull ye? Always sing, dinging Dame Grundy into my ears. What will Mrs Grundy zay? What will Mrs Grundy think . . . ?'

'My gosh,' Lofty said, 'I could think of a lot of people I'd like to do that to.'

He merrily chuckled away—with somewhat malicious undertones, I thought—while I enlightened him about Hardwick House, where Queen Elizabeth the First stayed (as where didn't she?) and Charles the First played bowls on the riverside green; Mapledurham House, which houses the Tudor Blount family and is hidden behind an avenue of elms which topple over one by one as members of the family die; and the house at Purley where Warren Hastings lived while he was awaiting his trial for impeachment. Then we came to Reading, where Lofty garaged his car ready for the rally next day, and I went home.

7

Rejoicing and Mourning at Reading

I

The name Reading means no more than that the place was the home of a man called Read (or Red). He was probably a tribesman of atrebate vintage who settled his family on the high ground between the Thames and the Kennet and by this sensible decision attracted other settlers of whom he became leader, thereby establishing the name.

There is plenty of archaeological evidence that there was a growing settlement there about the fourth century A.D., before the Anglo-Saxons' conversion to Christianity. But these settlers were easily unsettled when the Danes came. Though they were in a natural defensive position on high ground between the rivers they had evidently neglected to defend themselves from attack from the west. So when the Danes came sailing up the Thames in their square-sailed Viking ships, continued along the Thames when they came to the confluence with the Kennet, and sailed on westward, the Redingensians probably thought the invaders were out to capture the river crossing at Wallingford. A foolish conclusion. The Danes dropped anchor a mile or so upstream, swarmed ashore on the south bank, and went charging back eastward in full battle order. They were upon the settlement before anything could be done. They won the ground without difficulty and quickly fortified themselves by doing what the Redingensians should have done—by linking the Thames and the Kennet with a ditch and earthwork. They were thus ensconced on a triangle

K

of high ground and defended on all three sides by water. And they were to prove very troublesome to dislodge from there. The *Anglo-Saxon Chronicle* of the year 871 mentions battles galore for Reading—many of them led by King Alfred and his brother Ethelred—but from the fact that the place then disappears from recorded history for a couple of centuries one can assume only that it was devastated in battle and rebuilt after the Danes had been subdued.

By the time William the Conqueror ordered the compilation of his Domesday Book inventory ('We command therefore to know how the land is occupied and by what sort of men; what land we have of ourself, and what the archbishops and the diocesan bishops and the abbots and the earls, and what each man himself who is an occupier of land in England hath in land or in stock, and its worth in money'), there was plenty to record. Reading was a Hundred, a Manor, and a Borough (one of the only two in the county, Wallingford being the other). The King and the abbot of Battle, near Hastings, were joint lords of the manor and each held twenty-nine tenements and drew a hundred shillings in rents. The side of the valley where my house now stands was meadow, furrow, and wood. A few cattle grazed and pigs were herded among the trees. But industry had come too. The Thames and the Kennet were both turning flour mills.

However, it wasn't industry that raised Reading's stock: it was Henry the First's abbey, which was built on the site of the Danes' cantonment. There is a tale that Henry founded the abbey to contain the mummified hand of the apostle James, which tale, if true, could account for the human hand discovered in the ruins in 1786 and now kept in the Roman Catholic church of St Peter down river at Marlow. But the greater likelihood is that he founded it, as he said in its charter, for the salvation of his soul. Whatever its *raison d'être*, it was very large. It included two churches (one the size of Westminster Abbey), an hospitium with its own guest house and dormitory housing twenty-six poor people, a cemetery, an infirmary, a library, a mill, a refectory, a leper colony, stables, a chapter house, cellars, kitchens, the abbot's lodging (big enough in itself to need the attentions of forty servants), and extensive gardens. The monks were much given to brightening up their religious zeal with ceremony and music, and their clerk, John of Fornsete, probably composed one of the earliest extant pieces of English choral music, *Sumer is icumen in* ('Summer is a-coming in,/Loudly sing cuckoo,/Groweth seed and bloweth mead and sing'th the wood anew.–Sing cuckoo.') And no doubt the pastoral scenes in the river valley had much to do with the inspiration of the bucolic. But the first impressive non-military occasion in which the Thames figures in recorded history was the funeral of the abbey's founder.

Henry died at Angers in France on the 1st December 1135. His court at once made preparations for the funeral. His body was sewn into a bull's hide to preserve it, then carried in cortège to Cherbourg, where it was set upon a catafalque on the deck of the ship that was to take it to England. The sailing was delayed for three days because of storms in the Channel, but the ship and its escort eventually reached the Thames estuary on the 12th, anchored at Gravesend while organisation of the funeral convoy was completed, and began its progress up the Thames to Reading the following day.

From the records of the clerk whose job was to tot up the administrative expenses of the funeral it is clear that nothing was spared to bring the king's corpse home with proper ceremony. The pall draping the catafalque was of sable and Bayeaux velvet embroidered with the words HENRICVS : REX BRITT in purple and silver; the nobles standing vigil wore black velvet mantles over their armour; offices for the dead were sung throughout the voyage up the river by monks who had gone specially to meet the ship from Reading (for each psalm sung or office recited the King's treasurer paid out twelve shillings to the monastery); and at three places before reaching London Bridge the ship moored so that 'death alms' could be distributed to the poor—four pence to each recipient in coins that had been newly struck at Reading mint. It must have been a funereal progress indeed, for it rained continually from Gravesend to Reading. London Bridge and all the river-side wharves in the Pool were draped in black; solemn laments were played by the King's musicians when the monks weren't chanting their requiem lays; and the black and purple canopy protecting the catafalque had to be constantly changed and dried as the rain seeped through it and drenched out the sweal-ing candles that were supposed to be kept alight for the repose of the King's soul.

At Reading the abbey bells had been set tolling as soon as the news of Henry's death had come from France. Bishops from all over the country and abbots from all the Thames monasteries made journeys—some of them hazardous—to the abbey and were assembled at the quay when the funeral ship moored. The body was borne on a wagon pulled by six plumed and caparisoned horses. Muffled drums preceded and followed the cortège, and at the abbey gate heralds raised their trumpets and played a dirge. The abbey church was blazing with candlelight and the sacred relics—which in-cluded, besides St James's hand, St Philip's skull, one of St Luke's teeth, a piece of Moses' rod, and one of Christ's shoes —had been taken from the reliquary and stood in their gold caskets on the high altar.

When the final requiem mass had been said the scaffolders lowered the sarcophagus, the King's armour and accoutre-ments, and three urns containing water from the Ouse (Henry had been borne at Selby), the English Channel, and the Thames, into the tomb that had been opened in front of the altar. The bells continued to toll for three days, and on the river the barges that had brought the mourning dignitaries waited for their passengers, who were busy sandwiching their mourning between great feasts of funeral baked meats (veni-son, actually, brought up river from Windsor Park) and dis-cussions about the new king, Stephen. By the time the cere-monies were over, Stephen's downfall had been initiated. He was to suffer, and eventually fall, as the result of the spleen vented on him by barons who hated Henry's bureaucratic system even though they'd spent a week mourning its instigator. Mourning can cloak many nastier manifestations of human nature, as I scarcely need to remind you.

Rejoicing can too, as was demonstrated in the same setting in 1359, when Edward the Third married off the fourth of his sons, John of Gaunt, to Blanche of Lancaster.

The scenes then, in the abbey and the meadows bordering the river, were of a splendour unprecedented. The nuptial ceremony and mass lasted for seven hours, but the feasting and entertainment that preceded and followed them went on for ten days. Five hundred knights jousted in the arena in King's Meadow, but these jousts were only part of a tournament that included exhibitions of archery by the finest English longbowmen (they were so accurate in their aim that they could place their arrows in the interstices of plate armour), boat races on the river, wrestling matches, and minstrelsy contests. All these were watched by the king and the abbot, seated in a splendid pavilion that had been erected on the south bank of the Thames.

The minstrelsy contests were held in the evening when the light had failed and great fires were lit and kept fuelled from barges laden with faggots brought down river from Nuneham Park, where there was a forester who held the royal appointment of 'The King, of his Most Noble Majestie, his firer and faggoter'. And the king and the abbot were judges. Minstrelsy in the fourteenth century included the telling of tales as well as the singing of songs and the performance of instrumental music. Winners were selected in a series of heats in which the populace were entertained as they sat round fires and gradually eliminated contestants by demonstrations of their approval or disapproval. Finalists repeated their performances before the king and abbot, who chose the ultimate winners.

Of the tale-tellers, two who came to the royal pavilion were Simon Stede, an armourer who made a freelance income from minstrelsy, and Edouard Cloche, a professional troubador with sidelines in tumbling and patter. The tales they told are brief enough not to interrupt my story-line for an unconscionable time so I shall re-tell them. For reasons you will see in a moment, they were written down and kept.[1] This was Stede's:

A fisherman dwelling beside the river in Radynge came to his Curate in time of Lent and was confessed; and when his confession was in manner at the end, the Curate asked him whether he had any other thing to say that grieved his conscience, which, sore abashed, answered no word a great while.

At last, by exortation of his ghostly father, he said that there was one thing in his mind that greatly grieved his conscience, which he was ashamed to utter, for it was so grievous that he trowed God would never forgive him.

To whom the Curate answered and said that God's mercy was above all, and bade him not despair in the mercy of God, for, whatsoever it was, if he were repentant, God would forgive him.

And so, by long exortation, at the last he showed it, and said thus:

'Sir, it happened once, that as my wife was making a cheese on a Friday I would have said whether it had been salt or fresh, and took a little of the whey in my hand and put it in my mouth, and, or I was ware, part of it went down my throat against my will, and so I brake my fast.'

To whom the Curate said, 'If there be none other thing, I warrant God shall forgive thee.'

So when he had well comforted him with the mercy of God the Curate prayed him to answer a question and to tell him the truth.

The Curate said that there were robberies and murders done nigh Radynge, and divers men found slain and drowned in the Thames, and asked him whether he were consenting to any of them.

---

1. And, after Caxton had made the necessary arrangements, printed. They are collected into an anthology *A Hundred Merry Tales*, printed by Geoffrey Rastell, a brother-in-law of Sir Thomas More, in 1526.

To whom he answered and said 'Yes'; and said he was party to many of them, and did help to rob and to slay divers of them.

Then the Curate asked him why he did not confess him thereof.

The fisherman answered and said he took it for no sin, for it was a custom among them that when any booty came of any rich merchant riding, it was but a good neighbour's deed one to help another when one called another, and so they took that but for good fellowship and neighbourhood. And when such a neighbour asked him to watch for a certain rich man and find his purse and then to hide him in the deepest part of the river that he might reveal nothing of the robbery, he did so with a good heart and conscience, for he did indeed know where the deepest part of the river was and this knowledge he shared with the neighbour in good heart, as the neighbour shared the purse with him.

Here ye may see that some have remorse of conscience of small and venial sins, and fear not to do great offences without shame of the world or dread of God: and as the common proverb is, they stumble at a straw and leap over a block.

And this was Cloche's:

A young man late married to a wife thought it was good policy to get the mastery of her in the beginning.

Came to her, the pot seething over the fire, although the meat therein was not cooked enough, suddenly commanded her to take the pot from the fire.

Which answered and said, that the meat was not ready to eat.

And he said again, 'I will have it taken off, for my pleasure.'

This good woman, loth to offend him, set the pot beside the fire as he bade.

And anon after he commended her to set the pot beside the door, and she said thereto again, 'Ye be not wise herein.'

And she gently again did his commandment.

This man, yet not satisfied, commanded her to set the pot ahigh upon the hen-roost.

'What!' quoth the wife again; 'I trow ye be mad.'

And he fiercely then commanded her to set it there, or else, he said, she should repent.

She, somewhat afeared to move his patience, took a ladder and set it to the roost, and went herself up the ladder, and took the pot in her hand, praying her husband then to hold the ladder fast, for sliding; which so did.

And when the husband looked up and saw the pot stand there on height he said thus, 'So now standeth the pot there as I would have it.'

This wife, hearing that, suddenly poured the hot pottage on his head, and said thus: 'And now ben the pottage there as I would have them.'

By this tale men may see that it is no wisdom for a man to attempt a meek woman's patience too far, lest it turn to his own hurt and damage.

The king and the abbot decided that these two tales were of equal merit and ordered that the prize—freedom from common taxes for a year 'so long as the winner playeth not at foot ball, hand ball, hockey, coursing, cock fighting or other idle games' (these were forbidden because fletchers and bowyers had been complaining that audiences for archery contests had been falling off)—be equally divided, each winner to have six months' tax-free living. An equable enough arrangement, one would have thought. But Cloche thought otherwise—no-one knows for certain why, but possibly because he resented an amateur muscling in on the profession. At all events, he pursued Stede later in the evening and pushed him into the Thames to drown—a nastily malicious borrowing of events in Stede's story which may have seemed a bit of black comedy to Cloche but was to be his downfall, for the evidence of the court scrivener's transcript of the tales was used against Cloche at his trial—at which he was found guilty.

A few years after everyone had finished rejoicing over John of Gaunt's wedding, the Thames and the Kennet froze over thickly enough at Reading for a great feast to be held on it. The abbot ordained that all the poor and feeble of the town should be invited to it and that they should be given as a post-prandial gift as much sea-coal as would keep them warm for one week. The coal was brought from Newcastle down the east coast and up the Thames as far as Maidenhead, where the ice prevented the passage of the barges any farther; and from there the burgesses of the town arranged for labour parties to trundle loads of the coal up the frozen river to the feast. It was stacked in pyramids on the ice, and the old enfeebled merrymakers had to make their own arrangements for transportation to their homes.

A contemporary record by the abbey clerk says that by night-fall feast, coal, and recipients had alike disappeared and that nothing remained upon the Thames but the stripped tables, the trestles that had held the hogsheads of ale; and the black splotches where the coal had lain. The feast had been a royal one and included hogs, venison, fish, 'pies of meat and fennel', roast swan from the abbey swannery, cheeses, cider, mead, and ale. Great fires were lit on the banks of the river to keep the feasters warm, and monks from the abbey and brothers from Greyfriars turned themselves into waiters for the occasion.

Soon after this, though, in 1400, the river became—and not for the first or last time—a bearer of disaster instead of coal and goodies for the old and frail. The stains left upon the ice might have been an omen. The Black Death, carried by the fleas of the black rat, which in turn travelled up from London in the holds of ships, spread itself in Reading. (In 1348 Parliament had translated itself here to dodge the out-break of plague in London, but this time there was no escape.

Parliament was forced to sweat it out in the capital.) In Reading the rats ran up from the river—which was the town's only sewer—along the gutters and into houses already infested with vermin. The abbey's hospitium was soon overflowing with agonised sufferers, and south of the town, on the Basingstoke road, a casualty camp was hurriedly built for the isolation of the growing number of infected. These were nursed by a band of widows specially employed and paid danger money that came from a hurriedly levied local tax. They were called 'plague widows' because they had lost their husbands in previous outbreaks and had presumably developed strongly resistant antibodies in their blood as a result of mild infection. But their seeming immunity was said to be due to more sinister causes : they were thought to be in personal touch with the devil and to have some power over him through sorcery. They knew perfectly well that, unless they were sharpish in leaving the district, when the outbreak had ended they would be rounded up and flung into the Thames—ostensibly 'to clean them of their contamination', but actually as an assurance that they wouldn't blackmail the burgesses into giving them riches to prevent them re-infecting the town at their pleasure.

One of them, Widow Shafto, earnt the sum—immense for those days—of forty pounds in nursing money and wisely took herself off to London, where she bought a house in the stews of Southwark and turned it into a brothel. In doing so she established a centre of infection for another disease—gonorrhoea. She died in 1426 after dividing her fortune of four hundred pounds among the seven clap-ridden whores who were in her employ at the time. The bossiest of these, Bessie Bell, then assumed command and continued the running of the brothel as a co-operative enterprise. It remained known as Widow Shafto's Whorehouse until late in the sixteenth century, when it was burnt to the ground by an arsonist who saw himself as a vigilante.

Guardians of public morals—whether self-appointed or not —have always found the river useful as a symbol of cleanliness. Blasphemers and utters of obscenities have often been forced to the river bank and there made to swill out their mouths with the flowing water. The diarists Pepys and Evelyn have both commented on this apparently common sight. But fanatical vigilantes have sometimes found it convenient to see the Thames not only as a symbolic detergent but also as a medium of the wrath of God visited on the unholy. As, for example, in 1564.

In that year there were nearly a score of bridges in Reading, some of them mere footbridges over streams that linked the two main rivers, but the principal ones, naturally, over the Thames. But whether mere or principal they were all in a state of extreme disrepair. This was a result of Henry the Eighth's dissolution of the monasteries. The abbey had always taken responsibility for the maintenance of roads and bridges, but now that there was no functioning abbey the responsibility fell on the crown and the merchant guilds who virtually ran the town. The guilds were heavily in debt because of the decline in trade resulting from the disappearance of the monks and their immense purchasing power, and the crown machinery for dealing with the maintenance of communications was inadequate.

Queen Elizabeth the First got things moving by having reports made to her by engineers, and from these she noted that the bridges 'are very ruinous, falling and in great decay for default of repairs and amendments of the same so that no passage can be made over the same bridges without great danger, as well of our Subjects as of horses, oxen and animals. . . . So the resort and access of our Subjects travelling to and from the said Borough of Reading is greatly diminished, as well to the great poverty of the Inhabitants as to the decay and ruin of divers houses'. It was many years, though, before repairs and reconstruction were completed; and in 1564 there was ample opportunity for the fanatically perceptive to see the wrath of God venting itself through the frailty of the works of man—in particular the frailty of one of the rotting wooden bridges at Caversham, which collapsed in the middle during a late winter storm.

The river had been running high and turbulently for some
days and the lower meadows were flooded. 'The river was
noisome, and so the storm,' wrote Robert Greycoates the
street-corner thunderer who'd got it into his head that he must
save the world by calling on the people in it to repent. 'I
moved abroad at evening, ringing at my bell to summon the
ungodly to come and hear of Gods words thru me. Some
came and some stayed, but most would be home not to be
troubled by the storm, which was great. I went on past the
Grey Friars and to the river, and there set my brazier of coals
and carried it on my head to the river, meaning somewhat to
cross and continue afar, for I sometimes think Reading is without means to leave sin. And at the end of the bridge there was
crossing a man with cattle, and coming to from the other side
were many lanthorns and huzzahs that meant, I believed,
soldiers taking the night watch. It was dark and I stood
calling Repent Repent as the servant of God, but none would
hear me here and I said to myself that I would go on. But
there was a sudden shrieking of wind and a greater noise than
any mortal soul could make or imagine, and lanthorns,
soldiers, cattle and all upon the bridge were flung by the
wrathful might of God into the river for the mighty punishment of sinful living, as I have but warned all I found in my
time; and the bridge swept away in the great tumult. And so
I went home,—meeting all the way some who fell upon their
knees and many who were full of idle wonder at the noise;
and I told them all what I had seen of the wrath of God for
their wickedness. And I stayd abroad till the morning came
and the bridge [was seen to be] gone and the river not diminished in wildness.'

Greycoates's gleeful triumph, full of implied 'I told you so's'
and 'serve you right's', was matched during the years of 1664
and 1665, when Ralph Foote, another Reading downster of
fornication, gambling, and other forms of sinful living, laid
trails of corn from the wharf to the houses of those he suspected of special wickedness. Since it was not in those days
known that rats conveyed bubonic plague, Foote can be

saddled with no more than the malicious wish to encourage the verminous infestation of the homes of the ungodly; but since 1664 and 1665 were the years of the Great Plague of London and there is no doubt whatever that the disease spread to Reading, it may well have been that Foote in effect played the Pied Piper in reverse and introduced an early form of bacteriological warfare. It is certain that there was no easy escape for people who lived in towns linked by rivers, for the rivers were the principal means of communication and they bore the boats that bore the rats that bore the fleas that bore the plague.

At all events, Foote went off his head—either through guilt or enthusiasm—and rampaged up and down the town identifying himself with God and claiming that he had visited the plague upon Reading for its sinfulness. Whether the thousands who died were specially sinful is impossible to prove (it seems likely that they were just normally human). But the end of Foote was that his ecstatic triumph was too much for his physical as well as his mental balance. He fell off the parapet of one of the Thames bridges, on which he was shouting and posturing apocalyptically, and was drowned.

Only a few years earlier, in 1643, during the Civil War, the same bridge had been the scene of a different kind of drama.

The Cromwell parliament was in London and the king's headquarters were in Oxford. Reading, between the two, was of great strategic importance. River-borne supplies to both capitals could be controlled from there; and the road from Oxford to the south crossed the Thames at Caversham. The masters of Reading could be masters of the situation.

The town was in the hands of Cromwell's men first. These abandoned their garrison when Charles led his army in on its way to London. The king left a small garrison of royalist troops in charge, marched on after spending some days in the town (the Corporation records wail about 'those great charges which are now laid upon the Borough concerning cloth, apparel, victuals and other things for His Majesty's army'), and had to retreat before reaching London.

He returned to Reading, appointed one of his best generals, Sir Arthur Aston, to the governorship of the town, increased the garrison to three thousand men and three hundred horses, and went back up river to Oxford. Aston fortified Reading with earthworks and the seventeenth-century equivalent of pillboxes, and did the best he could to train his three thousand soldiers, who were all amateurish, cowardly, and rebellious, to fight the Roundheads when the chance came. His task wasn't made any easier by the citizenry, who kept up a loud and indignant grumbling about the way they were being taxed to support the garrison and the hard times they were enduring through loss of trade. Their complaint was justified, but when they petitioned the king ('may it therefore please your majesty to take into your most princely consideration the miserable state of your petitioners, who, through the general distractions of the kingdom, the decay of trade, the daily charge of your majesty's army billeted upon us, and the miserable cry of the numerous poor, are so impoverished that most of your petitioners are scarce able to support themselves') he coldly replied that they must lend him another £2,000. But Aston managed to keep the civilians and soldiers more or less controlled (he had to discipline one or two looting soldiers by hanging them); he also managed to learn in advance of a Fifth Column plot to kidnap him, and to make a sortie against the Roundhead garrison across the river at Henley (it was beaten back with heavy losses).

Then his bigger troubles began.

Cromwell's leader, the Earl of Essex, besieged Reading with sixteen thousand infantry and three thousand cavalry. He crossed the river at Caversham—having vanquished the royalist outpost there without much trouble—and set up his camps in the meadows on the south side. His troops were scarcely less pusillanimous than Charles's, and a lot of them caught cold through living in the open during a cold snap in the spring weather, but gradually they advanced towards the fortified town and eventually opened fire on it.

Aston was immediately knocked out—not by bullet or cannon ball but by a stone that fell from the wall beside which he was standing. This bit of Mack Sennett farce put him out of action for the rest of the siege, but his deputy, a man named Fielding, took over command and fought back for several days. Then supplies of food and ammunition dwindled and Fielding was faced with the problem of getting someone out of the besieged town to appeal for more. (The additional problem of getting the supplies into the town, always supposing they were discoverable and available, was one that would have to be faced later.) He sent a young ensign named Rupert Flower, who not only managed to get through the enemy lines but also learnt that there was a royalist gunpowder magazine at Henley. He crossed the river by the Foote Bridge (what else could it have been called?) and reached the royalist enclave by noon next day, travelling part of the way overhead like a monkey through the trees of Caversham Park, above the heads of the besiegers' reserves, who were camped below. He reported Fielding's plight and was told to return at once with the news that ammunition and supplies would be sent up river in a barge which could be given the best possible chance of getting into the defenders' hands by diverting it at the junction with the Kennet, since the Roundheads were thinnest on the ground on that side of the town.

After being fed and watered, Flower set off on the return journey and got to Foote Bridge without trouble. But in his anxiety to accomplish his mission he unwisely began his swim across the river when there was still enough daylight for him to be seen. He was spotted by the patrol on the bridge, trapped, and tortured into revealing the supply route. The barge was captured and the defenders were now back to square one, minus. The king himself launched an attack on Reading in the hope of relieving the town, and, indeed, managed to get a boatload of barrels of gunpowder over the river; but it was too late: Fielding had surrendered. 'Once more', one historian says, 'the Thames had proved to be death as well as life to the town.'

III

It has also proved to be a useful escape route—not only for people pursued by doom but also for those trying to avoid lesser troubles.

King John was one of several monarchs who gave Reading permission to hold fairs to celebrate the feast days of saints— Saints Philip and James in his case. These fairs—like tourneys, festivals of games, and similar jamborees—were always held in King's Meadow on the south side of the Thames and were great public sprees, but for some people the pleasure of them was slightly diluted because they were also the recognised time for settling debts. Many a debtor confronted by his creditors at some stall or sideshow jumped into the river and swam downstream towards Sonning, which had in its church a special sanctuary for debtors bestowed by one of the early bishops of Salisbury, who had a winter retreat in the village.

Officially, the roads also offered a measure of safety, for John's father, Henry the Second, had decreed that travellers to and from fairs were to be given 'the King's peace'—that is, any attacks made on them en route would be regarded as personal attacks on the king and therefore punishable by death. But the river was safer anyway, because what happened in it would be seen by far more people and the king's peace implemented if necessary. Once outside 'the mannor of Reddynge' beaters-up of debtors were subject only to the normal laws—unless two adjacent manors were holding fairs simultaneously—so escapers made as fast as they could for Sonning and the sanctuary. One such is said to have run into the church once, sodden and covered with weed and slime, when King John himself was paying a non-ceremonial visit and was in the middle of a quiet prayer. The confrontation of king and peasant was taken as the subject of a picture by Holman Hunt

—he who painted *The Light of the World*—but he thought better of it and abandoned it at the sketch stage. Hunt was himself a resident of Sonning and it seems probable that he intended the painting as a gift to the church. Perhaps he gave money for one of the frequent restorations instead.

An escape to Sonning from the other direction, and for different reasons, was made by Queen Isabella, the second wife of Richard the Second, who came at night up the Thames from Windsor and was given sanctuary in the episcopal retreat while Henry of Lancaster was forcing his cousin to abdicate so that he himself could become Henry the Fourth, which he did.

Isabella wrote to her host and succourer that his goodness and kindness, Godly though they were, 'could have come to nothing without the aid of this sweet river that bore me safe from the prying eyes of mine enemies and the King his enemies who are the same, and of God allso the enemies; and it is therefore of your beneficence that I pray, for the river and for me and for the king my husband'. It was evidently as usual in those days as now, when in a state of emotional stress, to give a big build-up to a superficial cause of gratitude. The river could hardly have had much to do with the fact that her escape was unhampered; all the same, various parts of the stretch from Sonning down to Windsor were known, until well into the sixteenth century, as 'Isabella's blessing'. Which is a pleasant conceit.

And talking of conceits, I discovered another one at Shiplake, the next village downstream, when I went there on a planned sightseeing tour. (Planned sightseeing is not an activity I favour, but, like boarding-house cabbage and Beatles, is part of the rich pageant of life and should be sampled—even if with a preliminary shudder.) The Shiplake sights are all of the self-consciously nurtured variety—gardens 'landscaped' and maintained immaculate under contract, poodles owned by stockbrokers' wives and encumbered with jewelled collars, pubs with transitory tarts drinking Bloody Marys paid for by escorts wearing silk cravats, new punts moored at the river bank and piled high with coloured scatter-cushions that will make pretty Kodachromes but are never likely to be lounged on by punted girls, and a modern church that pretends to be old. All these and a wodge of similarly twee sights I had observed without thinking them worth noting here, except as a parenthetical catalogue, when my guide showed me the ultimate in tweeness.

He was a rich dark man, like a fruit cake, who eked out a frenetic existence between a boardroom and what he called his 'Thames cottage' (it had six acres of landscaped garden, a heated swimming pool, an electric barbecue, a garage for four cars, and a pagan temple he'd translated brick by brick from Druid country somewhere because he thought it would be 'nice for cavorting couples'). Naturally he had a cabin cruiser with a cabin panelled in rich woods and it was this, his newest toy, that he made the climax of our tour of what he called 'my hideaway from the rat-race, the sweetest village in *this jewel set in the silver sea*'. He carefully italicised the words for me then added, 'You know Shakespeare?'

'I know the line you mean,' I told him.

'Yes. Well, this'—he made a proprietorial gesture embracing all the visible Thames—'is *my* silver sea. And I've set a jewel in it for posterity. I'll show you.'

From a bunch of impressive keys slung to the waist of his vicuña slacks by a gold chain he selected one that opened a safe tucked away behind a bit of the rich panelling. From inside the safe he took a casket of black crocodile (Asprey? Cartier?); and from inside this he took a smaller casket. 'Fireproof,' he explained.

The suspense was of course terrific, but he wasn't going to skip the build-up just because globules of anticipatory sweat were glistening on my forehead.

'The great Poet Laureate, Alfred Lord Tennyson, was married in the village church here, you know.'

Pause to let me grasp the magnitude of this fact.

'His wife's name was Emily Sellwood—before she married him of course.'

'Of course,' I agreed.

'What a marvellous man he must have been! He actually wrote a poem in the carriage they drove away from the church in! Isn't that wonderful? No normal man could do that. You or I couldn't.'

'Even if I could have I wouldn't have on that occasion,' I said. 'Fiddling about with poems while the rice is still pattering on the roof and your bride probably needs comforting with a drop of the blushful Hippocrene. A hip flask would be the thing to fiddle with.'

'Eh? I don't think you're quite with me. This is one of the most lovely poems in the English language.' He down-decibelled his voice until it was scarcely louder than the river lapping against the boat. 'It's called "Marriage Morning".'

'Oh, that one,' I said—with, I must admit, an overtone of scorn, *Marriage Morning* being in my view one of the worst poems ever written. Fortunately he mistook my scorn for enthusiasm, held up a finger for silence, and selected another key for the inner casket. I took it he was about to produce the the manuscript of *Marriage Morning* and I prepared to make the right sort of noises. What he in fact took out was one of those tiny tubes that one attaches to dogs, umbrellas, and other loseable gadgets, and which contain a rolled up bit of paper bearing the owner's name and address. This one, however, contained *Marriage Morning* typed by an electric typewriter on India paper and headed 'The Most BEAUTIFUL poem in the ENGLISH language'. Since four of its best lines are

> Oh, the woods and the meadows,
> Woods where we hid from the wet;
> Stiles where we stayed to be kind,
> Meadows in which we met

I couldn't agree. But I thought his gimmickry just about summed up Shiplake and all who live in her.

Wargrave, downstream a little on the other side of the river, is going to get even shorter shrift from me. But I shall mention the narrative of an acquaintance of mine, a rumbustious fellow called Tom Perkins, who was in both the world wars and now divides his time between night portering at a London club and lunchtime waiting in a restaurant. He was born in Wargrave and told me, more or less as follows, of his exciting time in 1914: 'Prepared me for a lot of the horrors of war, it did. I was on the Somme, but it never seemed to me so bad as it was written about, and I think that was because I'd had this experience.

'Nineteen-fourteen, it was. I was only a lad—eighteen, I'd be—and I was having me dinner one day when someone came to the back door and told Mother someone'd have to go for Heather, the bobby—we hadn't got one in Wargrave, you see, Heather lived in Sonning—because a woman'd have to be arrested.

' "Not my Tom," Mother said—thinking it was an easy virtue lady, I suppose, and knowing I didn't know about such things—which I didn't, we were all innocent much longer in those days—"my Tom's not getting mixed up with such. Heather's got a telephone now, let someone speak on that." But no, nothing would do but that I must go, and of course I was itching to get away. I had a bike and I 'xpect I saw m'self as a hero rushing off for rescue.

' "But what's this woman *done* ?" Mother said. She couldn't think of a thing a woman could do and be arrested for unless it was sex, see? Pure as the driven snow, she was, but suspicious when it came to protecting her one and only—that's me.

'Anyway, this woman that had come to the door to get me—I'll think of her name in a minute—she suddenly said : "*Done?* She pushed a lot of flaming rags in the pillar-box and set fire to the letters, that's what she's done."

'It was one of those suffragettes, see? I 'xpect you've heard how they went about chaining themselves to railings, falling in front of horses and so on—then hunger striking when they got jailed? Yes. Well, we'd heard all about them in Wargrave, but this was the nearest one had got to us. I was riled because there was a letter of mine in that pillar-box—I'd written to the

Boy's Own Paper—and I remember thinking I'd have to do it all over again, not to mention the stamp.

'Anyway, off I went and fetched Heather—to cut a long story short—and he came and arrested this woman. She hadn't tried to get away or anything, she was just standing there with a bit of a crowd round her and holding a placard which said "Votes for Women". You can imagine what a rumpus there was in the village—we hadn't had so much excitement since Mafeking.

'But there was far more to come. They were cunning, those suffragettes. The pillar-box fire was just to draw fire, so to speak—put us off our guard. They knew we'd be too busy talking about a small incident to worry about watching for a bigger one. Very crafty.

'Because next thing was, they set fire to the *church*. A party of them came to the village pretending to be just sightseers and set fire to the *church*. Well, I mean! I'm not much for God-bothering, but you've got to draw the line somewhere.

'Well, there was a real panic, and of course we hadn't any fire engine nearer than Reading. We phoned for help and then started a chain of buckets from the river. I was a link in the chain and I never worked so hard in my life. Much good it did us. It was like putting out Rome with teacups. The whole place was blazing like a madman's holiday by the time Reading came. They had a horse engine with a hand pump and lengths of hose that spurted fountains at the joins—it was like one of those aquatic displays at the Alhambra. Everyone was helping. I was rushing about putting buckets over the leaks and getting drenched. It was a dry night and you could hear the pews crackling like kindling. The suffragettes had been caught and arrested, but there was too much for the Black Maria to do and too much for the bobbies to do too, and they couldn't do anything but handcuff the six of them together round a lamp-post, where they kept up a sort of ring-a-roses, shouting about votes for women. Them and their bloody votes for women! There wasn't a woman in the village that night who wouldn't have dotted them one. Nobody'd thought much about the church before, except as some-where you had to go to on Sunday mornings or you'd be looked down on—and get a good drubbing from the vicar into the bargain. But now it was alight and dam' near setting the whole village alight, that was different. Well, naturally.

'Then the business of the graves came up. We had two famous ones—Madame Tussaud and Thomas Day. Young fellers used to punt their girls up the river and take them in the churchyard and show them old Tussaud. "Heah, may deah," they used to say, "rests th' bodday of Madarm Tooso, who during the French revolooshon used to—ah—peel death masks orf heads recently—ah—*gee*oteened." A cheerful sort of subject for a courting couple, I must say. But they always did this little lecture. Then they used to show Tom Day's grave—he was a writer, years dead, who wrote a book, *Sandford and Merton*, and whether these lads had read it or not they used to kid their girls they had. "Deah old *Sandford and Merton*," they used to say, and pat Tom on the epitaph.

'Well, these graves were getting trampled on well and truly with all the activity going on. Nobody seemed to care about any of the other poor old corpses—but these two famous ones had to be protected from all the debris falling about. So you know what they did? They unhitched the suffragettes from round the lamp-post and laid 'em on the graves. They never even bothered to get up. They was martyring themselves a bit more, see? Their clothes got set light to by sparks and they rolled about a bit to douse the flames, but that was all. You could hear 'em shouting "Votes for women, votes for women" above all the ruddy uproar. And they got drenched with the water being pumped up from the river by the fire engine. People just took it as a matter of course, and when the fire was put out—the church was a write off—they were still there, laying on old Madame Tussaud and Tom Day, and some of the village people kept chucking buckets of river water over them to show how they felt. Which is about the only time the old river's been used as a reviver for vote-drunk women, I'll warrant.'

8

Hellfire and Regatta

I

POSSIBLY. But the Thames has been used many a time as a reviver for ordinary drink-drunks. Lovelace wasn't the only one who found it an allaying balm. And the stretch in which the widest assortment of drunks has been dunked to recover is from Henley down to Hambledon Lock—a couple of miles in which thick heads have spluttered on many recorded occasions, particularly since 1786.

That was the year the bridge was built. And the labourers and stonemasons who sank its caissons and carved its balustrades were a rambunctious lot whose boozy propensities were mightily encouraged by the local tale of the invention of bottled beer. This tale is about a Dean of St. Paul's—he was a real dean, Alexander Nowell—who had come down to Henley for a little peaceful fishing. He had used the Red Lion inn as his headquarters, but his visits there to slake his thirst were so numerous that he asked the landlord for a supply of ale in a vessel so that he could, as he put it, 'fish and quench without constant recourse to the wearying business of having to march to the inn to replenish one's ale, thereby making the thirst and the quenching thereof a *continuum ad nauseam*'.

The only vessel the landlord could find was a demijohn with a stopper, and into the narrow neck of this he funnelled a gallon of ale and corked it tightly. The dean drank another gallon in the pub as a foundation, then returned to the river with his demijohn. Not surprisingly, he fell asleep. He woke up hours later with a great thirst and a cloudy head. The demijohn forgotten, he groped his way back to the pub with his fishing tackle. Next day he had to visit his bishop and later other business intervened and he was unable to get on with his fishing for several days. When at last he returned to his favourite spot he found the demijohn still there hidden in the grass. But by now the natural gas in the beer had built up, and when he uncorked he found he had 'not a bottle but a gun, by the sound thereof, and a great spouting into the air of the ale in a foam; but a good taste thereto, when the foam subsided'.

The bridge builders, not unnaturally, seized on this tale as an imprimatur for their drinking habits. When reproached, as they often were by zealous upholders of Henley's dignity, they made out a good case for upholding the importance of the invention of bottled beer by drinking more of it to the glory of the place where it was invented. When they were paid they went on rowdy carousals and finished up lying on the river banks in rows with their thick heads lapped by the water. On each of these occasions they would appoint one of their number who agreed not to exceed moderate drinking, or was particularly hard-headed, as a 'watcher', and he would be responsible for anchoring the supine bodies by their ankles to trees or blocks of masonry so that they couldn't slip down the bank into the river.

Anne Damer, a sculptress cousin of Horace Walpole, wrote that 'on high days and holy days the banks are scattered like a ninepin floor with the drunken men who build our bridge. But between these riots of the fleshly pleasures they are sober and strong and perform marvels of their strength, lifting the blocks into position.' When the bridge was almost finished she carved effigies of Tamesis and Isis on the keystones of the central arch, and I find it pleasing to imagine—there is not a shred of evidence to support my imagination—that she meant them as symbolic watchers over the drunken sleeps of the men she so admired.

In 1809 the river flooded into the town and overacted its

restorative powers on a couple of drunks who had no benevo-
lent power watching over them—carved or otherwise. These
had emerged from a pub in fine bibulous fettle and decided
—as one of them was heard telling the landlord, who reported
it in the evidence at the subsequent inquest—'to shlake first
of theet in the sea'. In his efforts to take off his boots and
socks to slake the thirst of his feet he fell in the flood water and,
singing lustily, dragged his companion down with him. Both
were drowned, and the bodies were not recovered until three
days later when the floods subsided.

Equally disastrous but more ghoulish is the case reported
by Lawrence Medcalf, an itinerant preacher who had completed an evangelistic campaign in Henley in 1822 and was
on his way east to Marlow when he came upon the naked and
apparently dead body of a man lying in Remenham Wood, just
across the river. Since to the innocent all things are innocent and
there was clotted blood round a wound in the man's chest, he
assumed he had found a foot-pad's victim. He hastily said some
suitable prayers and returned to Henley to report the matter.
Soon after his departure the drunk recovered—the 'wound' was
no more than the puncture of a thorn, sustained in falling—and
recalled vaguely that he had left his clothes somewhere by
the river before taking a reviving dip. Keeping to the woods,
he made off unsteadily—but in the wrong direction. He got
completely lost and was wandering about the woods for hours.
He was seen about midnight by one of the party of coroner's
men Medcalf had brought to recover the body, and this man,
taking him for a spectre, ran back to Henley screaming blue
murder and subsequently had an hysterical apoplexy from
which he died.

(The wood in which all this to-do went on was, by the
way, part of Park Place, which George the Second's son
Frederick—'Poor Fred'—made his home for a while. Frederick died before his father, and his son, the future George the
Third, became heir apparent at the age of thirteen. He chose
Park Place because it had 'the royal dignity of the best river
in England as its boundary, and the ghost of that wretched

Stuart, Charles, haunts the Red Lion inn'. Charles the First did in fact stay at the inn in 1632, but Frederick's seems to be the only reference to any ghost. George the Third's Secretary of State, Field-Marshal Conway, bought Park Place and planted the first poplars in England along the river bank as a tribute 'to Frederick, Prince of Wales, who loved the river hereabouts'.)

The river at Henley really came into its own as a power for the assuagement of hangovers in 1829, when the first Oxford and Cambridge boat race was held there. Cambridge wore pink sashes round woolly vests on this occasion, but their choice of a cheerful colour (in honour of their President, a man named Snow) brought them no luck and Oxford, favouring their sombre dark blue, won. Other people's boat-race parties are boring to read about, and the ones held by the crews and their supporters on this occasion are no exception; but the landlord of the Red Lion 'was kept busy all the night helping young gentlemen of our Mother Universities, who in their enthusiasm for both losers and winners had imbibed unwisely but too well and were continually needing lanthorn men to guide them to the river, where they went swimming to refresh themselves and cure their aching heads'.

The boat race was never held at Henley again (it wasn't repeated at all until 17th June 1836, when the course was from Westminster to Putney), but in 1839 came the establishment of the annual regatta, since when there has been a matching annual succession of regatta parties in all degrees of social distinction.

Hone's *Everyday Book* records, typically, in 1867 : 'Once more the splendid occasion of the Royal[1] Regatta at Henley-on-Thames has come and gone. The grace of the ladies and the dignity of the gentlemen, and the endurance of the competitors in these delightful events that so become the days of King Sol, has been noteworthy. Parasols, laces and ribbons and furbelows of every variety, uniforms, swords, elegant

1. The prefix stuck after the Prince Consort watched all the main events in 1851 and told Queen Victoria he was 'well pleased'.

cravats, and all the sartorial modes of the day have been evident on every hand. No day has passed without its bevy of beauty on parade for the world and his wife to see and envy. The humble have admired the accoutrements of the wealthy, and the upper classes have gentled the lower with smiles. Our Fatherly Thames has flowed softly in silvern beauty down the Reach, his gentle ripples cleft by the boats and rhythmically agitated by the oarsmen, and each day King Sol has smiled his benefice. Each night has (and some will say regrettably) seen ruder activities. We mean the customary onset of intoxication that the lower orders in particular seem to delight in, though many of them are forever seeking charity. Innkeepers of the rougher kind encourage such conduct, without doubt; nonetheless it is scarcely to the advantage of a Royal Occasion that this year *as so often before* the beauty of the Thames has been sullied by riotous bands of rough men (and, save the mark, a few of the gentler sex!) who make no ado about throwing each other bodily into the water in search of coolth when they are over-heated by grape and grain.

'Our Watcher counted as many as a score within the hour between eleven and midnight o'clock on a single evening. Their rude singing and calling made things most unpleasant for gentlemen of superior breeding who also had come to the river, though only to bathe their faces as a curative for tiredness after the long day's festivities. A uniformed policeman moved the rough ones on from time to time, but their intoxicated state made them difficult and abusive, and our Watcher was told that to take them in charge would have been useless as the prison house was full.' No doubt the water was equally effective for both tired gentlemen and drunken loafers, since both were hung over; but our Watcher sounds to me like the same man that wrote 'horses sweat, gentlemen perspire, ladies acquire a gentle glow'. He was clearly a man for social distinctions.

Social distinctions still prevail on the banks of the river at regatta time; it is an occasion like Ascot. But no-one nowadays is denied the solace of a river recovery, whether his party has been champagne or beer; and the booms and barriers that mark the course are often to be seen being clung to in the early hours of the morning by both top and bottom people.

II

Any of them would have fulfilled one of the two qualifications for membership of the Hellfire Club, an eighteenth-century institution renowned for unspeakable practices about which I shall write a few contemptuous words. Nominees had to have been seen by all the other members 'in a state of helpless insobriety'—that was the first qualification. The other was that one had to have visited Italy, and this kept the social status mainly top drawer. Reactionary opinion, beginning in the later years of the century to horrify itself at the low moral standards of an age that had in fact been remarkable for other things than Gin Lane squalor—among them, wit—seized on the Hellfire Club as a symbol of utter decadence and turned out accusatory reams in which the phrases 'nameless orgies' and 'sinister practices' cropped up as often as Ouches in a Billy Bunter story. The Club flourished on these injections of wickedness and held its orgies, such as they were, on the site of Medmenham Abbey, four miles down stream from Henley.

The Abbey, a small one already in a seedy state by the time of the Dissolution, was finished off with the rest of the monastic institutions. The records of a long-defunct group of potamologists called The Thames Historiographers say that 'hereabouts the river was defiled by the most frightful slaughter and ran red with the blood of the misfortunate monks, who had earned nothing but gratitude for their charity, yet were minced and thrown to the fishes'.

There were only two monks in residence at the time, so there couldn't have been all that much slaughter; but the founder of the Hellfire Cub, Sir Francis Dashwood, was no doubt thrilled to the innermost fibres of his schoolboy mind by this gory comment. He found a couple of kindred spirits in Charles Churchill, a rubbishy poet, and Paul Whitehead, an unendearing character who married an imbecile girl so that he could inherit her fortune and support himself in style above his station and write mildly pornographic plays. One of the rules of invitation into the club was that initiates should 'quaff from a skull a gallon of Thames water bloodied by the slaughtered Cistercians and toast their agonised death with glee'. In two hundred years the blood must have become somewhat weakened by the water; but no doubt the symbolism was the thing. The members of the club called themselves monks, adopted a motto, 'Do as you like',[1] intoned the Lord's Prayer backwards (with what object the Lord knows), held feasts, imposed curses, and danced naked in the moonlight. This seems to have been the sum of their wickedness and it sounds pretty dull to me. But you still find breath being bated when utterances about them are made.

The members of the Hellfire Club, when boating down from London for their piffling little orgies, always stopped at Hurley, a mile short of Medmenham, to change into their monks' habits and have an aperitif. They used Ladye Place, a house once owned by the Richard Lovelace of the allaying balm. (It was used also by later Lovelaces, the enemies of James the Second, as a venue for their plot to ensure the succession of William of Orange.) Lovelace was a romantic, a Cavalier who was imprisoned for cavaliering, and a minor lyric poet two of whose phrases are among the most famous in literature ('Stone walls do not a prison make,/Nor iron bars a cage' and 'I could not love thee, Dear, so much,/Loved I not Honour more'). He was a great Thames lover but eventually he was forced to sell his estates and leave Ladye Place. He went to live in London and took with him a phial of Hurley water which, as he wrote to a friend, 'could scarce be more loved by me as a memorial of the pastoral I loved, had

1. They adopted it in Latin, 'Fay ce que vondras' to make it more impressive.

I trapped it in rare Venetian. But it is as ghostly as she of
Bisham.'

The lady of Bisham he referred to was Lady Hoby, famous
as a ghost and as the sadistic originator of the tag 'He blotted
his copy book'. Her family was given the fourteenth-century
abbey there by Mary Tudor—a suitable donor, considering
the bloody deed that took place by the river. Lady Hoby set
great store by learning (she was herself remarkably well
educated for a sixteenth-century woman) and she had a small
son who was slow-witted and untidy. She tried literally to beat
his lessons into him; but this, understandably, only made him
neurotic and cowering and his work grew worse. The blots in
his lesson books aroused her to such dreadful anger that eventually she beat him to death. The scene of this final murderous
assault was the lawn that ran down to the river from the
house. At the edge there was a bower used as a schoolroom,
and the villagers who were continually passing along the towpath on the opposite bank had often seen the woman be-
labouring the boy; but they could of course do nothing but
touch forelocks or curtsey, she being a lady of quality. One of
them, however, said in the inn that he had 'seen this day My
Lady's boy being bludgeoned about the head till he collapsed
on the ground with the blood running from eyes and nose and
ears till the grass itself turned red'.

Lady Hoby is said to have haunted the abbey after her own
death, wringing her hands and crying out her repentance; and
as the house is still standing the legend of the ghost goes on.
The villagers are very fond of telling tourists about it. I found
no-one who'd actually seen the ghost, but the blotted copy
books were discovered in a bureau drawer when men were
working in one of the attics in 1840. 'The sanguine stains of
blood as well as ink were upon them still,' the Victorian
Commonplace Book of a local resident records.

I don't know whether this grim little story over-sensitised
me, but I felt dismal all the way from Bisham to Marlow—
a good half mile. Perhaps it was the graveyards beside the
river (Bisham's includes Warwick the Kingmaker, who

blotted *his* copy book at the battle of Barnet in 1471;
Marlow's includes Edgar Wallace), or the unpleasing appearance of the mummified hand of the alleged St James in the
Catholic church; or perhaps it was the thought of Shelley and
his wife slogging away in their rooms in West Street, Marlow,
at *Frankenstein* (hers) and *The Revolt of Islam* (his)—both
somewhat disspiriting works. Or it could have been that I had
a sudden rush to the head of sympathy for Shelley, whose
pressing creditors eventually drove him away from the river
he liked to boat on and about which he remarked to Thomas
Love Peacock, 'It runs with the blood and bones of a thousand
heroes and villains, and no doubt the water is sour with
tainting; but the scene is most satisfactory, you must agree.'

III

The scene a little farther down, at Cliveden Reach, between
Cookham and Maidenhead, is satisfactory indeed. More
writers than I care to compete with in ecstasy have written
about it in glowing terms. But scenes that attract ecstatic
writers attract ecstatic non-writers too—many of them to gawp
in clockwork response at what they have been told is the most
beautiful stretch of the Thames. Out of gratitude they add to
the beauty of the scene a continual votive outpouring of background music from their transistor radios, and their own
comments rich in the natural beauty of words—for example,
'innit *gorg*eous, innit smashing?' 'I reckon them trees is a
bloody sight older'n you'll ever get.' 'All right, I s'pose. I like
a bit more glamour, a bitter life, night clubs, all that.' 'Them
fields is pretty, innem?'

From here on, right down to Windsor, the river seems to
be burdened also with a concentrated allocation of people who
are neither interesting nor attractive. They seem to me to be
more a special species of non-people about whom there is little
to be said except that while here they are uninteresting because

they are interested in nothing. Presumably they lead lives somewhere. But the river has on them the effect of some neutralising agent. They dine at expensive riverside hotels, glide up and down in expensively hired launches, put on yachting caps and Bermuda shorts and chunky sweaters, wear dresses designed by Mary Quant apparently for some festival of goons, and bleat to each other with all the passion of rheumatic sloths. They take nothing and they give nothing. The only reason for their mention here is to herald the chapter on the stretch from Cliveden to Windsor, which seems to be peculiarly their bailiwick.

9

The Hymen of London

THERE have been two good houses at Cliveden, one built in
the seventeenth century for the Duke of Buckingham, the
other designed by the architect of the Houses of Parliament,
Sir Charles Barry, for the Duke of Westminster and built in
1850. This is still there and now belongs to Lord Astor.
The earlier house was another riverside home of 'Poor Fred',
and John Evelyn wrote about the formal gardens: 'I went to
Clifden, that stupendous natural rock, wood and prospect of
the Duke of Buckingham's, buildings of extraordinary expense.
The grotts in the chalky rock are pretty: 'tis a romantic
object, and the place altogether answers the most poetical
description that can be made of solitude, precipice, prospect
or whatever can contribute to a thing so very like their
imaginations. The stande, somewhat like Frascati as to its
front, and, on the platform, is a circular view to the utmost
verge of the horizon, which with the serpenting of the Thames
is admirable. The staire case is for its materials singular; the
cloisters, descents, gardens, and avenue thro' the wood, august
and stately, but the land all about wretchedly barren, and
producing nothing but ferne. Indeede, as I told his Majesty
that evening (asking me how I liked Clifden) without flattery,
that it did not please me so well as Windsor for the prospect
and park, which is without compare, there being only one
opening, and that narrow, which led one to any variety, where-
as that of Windsor is every where greate and unconfin'd.'

M

When Frederick had the place he held a right royal fête on
the river and watched it from a seat at the top of the balust-
raded steps rising from the water's edge. There were fireworks,
string bands playing background music in the gardens, solo
singers and instrumentalists who performed at the foot of the
steps with a net held behind them in case their fervour caused
them to step back too far, and, as a grand finale, a performance of the masque-opera *Alfred*. This paid somewhat unctuous
tribute to 'the King of this mighty river and of the realms
astride it, your mighty ancestor, father of England' in a
series of richly designed scenes that passed on barges before
the Prince. *Alfred* had music by Thomas Arne, and a script
by two hack poets, James Thomson and David Mallet.
Thomson had a pension of a hundred pounds a year from the
Civil List because he had once replied to Frederick's inquiry
about the state of his affairs, 'They are in a more poetical
posture, Sir, than formerly.' If the Prince thought this a gem
of wit he is unlikely to have noticed that the words of *Alfred*
were awful. He told Thomson that the closing scene was the
climax of 'The finest contrived of all masques', and rose en-
thusiastically to applaud. The supernumeraries of the chorus,
hidden with the musicians among the garden hedges, oblig-
ingly repeated the final song, and it's been repeated a good
many times since. It was *Rule, Britannia*.

As the night was so fine and the singing of this chauvinistic
twaddle so lusty it may well be that it was heard two miles
farther down at Maidenhead—a place aptly named for a first
performance. Michael Arlen said that Maidenhead was the
hymen of London, but that it was scarcely worth rupturing
as there were better ways in. This is true now—the town is
but merely a place for skittish wickedness for the non-people
I mentioned a couple of pages ago. But it has had its interesting
and dramatic moments. It was a hythe, or wharf, in the tenth
century and remained one until the seventeenth. Charles the
First, in the charge of a posse of Cromwell's men, landed there
in 1647 and was escorted up to the Greyhound Inn, where

he touchingly said goodbye to his children before his final imprisonment. He stood on the wooden bridge and remarked that the weather was icy and that the timbers creaked with age. 'I hope someone will see to it,' he added, 'that my bounty of trees continue.' He was referring to a grant in perpetuity originally made by Henry the Fourth for three trees a year to be supplied from the forest in the Royal Manor of Bray for the maintenance of the bridge, which carried the main road to the west over the river and remained in use until 1776, though the new stone one which is there now was built in 1772. To the south of it that remarkable engineer Brunel, who thought rivers 'the only truly worthy adversaries' and was tunnelling beneath the Thames when he was only nineteen, built a splendid bridge to carry the Great Western railway line. In 1844 the equally remarkable painter Turner set up temporary shop in Maidenhead and with Brunel's bridge as his model made his studies for the painting which expressed the impact of the steam age on his marvellous imagination— *Rain, Steam and Speed.*

The modern wickedness of the town about which the non-people nudge each other so coyly is about as invigorating as the Hellfire Club's. There are one or two places where tycoons who have lunched in London take their popsies for dinner and bed; there are strings of coloured lights at night; night clubs with implications of pornography that alas are never fulfilled; and a few private rooms where lechery unbounded is said to go on. I expected to see some startling *graffiti*, but the only one I saw was 'Keep the Red Flag Flying High' on the wall of a pub. The non-men lounge in the lounges checking that the Durex are safe in their wallets, while in the Powder Rooms the non-women complete that utmost in devilishness, the removal of their pants, before leaving for the ferny beds of Maidenhead Thicket. (Highwaymen used to lie low here, waiting for the London coaches, and possibly theirs was the last bit of real lawlessness ever to be perpetrated round Maidenhead.) All the spurious glamour that encroaches on the

Thames hereabouts is a degeneration, I think, of the romanticism that was part of the Edwardian era and was over-exploited by, in the main, the boys of Eton. I spoke with one Old Etonian who told me :

'The thing about the river at Maidenhead is that it's got a shingly bed. This means that it's the best spot for punting. You avoid all the embarrassment of getting your pole stuck in the mud, and there are plenty of shady trees to moor under. We used to wear blazers and straw hats, of course, and if you were in funds and could do the job properly you had a hamper from Fortnum's and something to play the Eton Boating Song on. With me, it was a concertina, but there was one fellow I remember who always took a portable harmonium. The best thing was a flute or whistle of some kind, which gave the tune a quality it doesn't possess of itself. The girls used to love it— I think they found it the epitome of romance. Any summer weekend you could pick up the strains all the way from Windsor to Cliveden. If we passed one another in punts there was a rule—unwritten of course—that we should take off our boaters and screen our faces with them. The girls would screen themselves with their parasols. In this way we could play the gentlemanly game of complete ignorance of identity. Nobody ever saw anybody personally.

'The tempo of courtship was much slower in those days. You weren't on top of the girl before she'd finished her first drink. I suppose we had a better developed sense of drama and wanted the climax at the proper place—the end. And the end was engagement or marriage. Girls did get laid of course, but as a general rule we did the gentlemanly thing and contained ourselves. As a result, a kind of coy legend of wickedness was always lurking in the background. Naturally nothing was ever said, but it was inferred that if you were at Eton you were sophisticated and had to become "a man of the world"—marvellous phrase!—and therefore had to have a masculine private life which had the lid of respectability shut tight on it. This inference had what we'd call today a subliminal effect and in time a demand arose for something that wasn't really needed but had been thrust upon us, as it were. And Maidenhead was the place. Windsor was nearer but the thought of a brothel in Windsor, where the royal family lived, would have been too shocking for words.

'I think it was this thought of the proximity of royalty that always made even the wickedness away down river in Maidenhead a bit halfhearted. And anyway you had to be surreptitious. The hotels were places where you were seen with girls of your own class—the girls you punted on the river and invited to the Fourth of June. But the others—"girls of a *certain* class" as the euphemism had it—weren't to be seen with at all. Damn it, you might leave Eton and go up to Oxford or Cambridge and come down and join the Guards or the church or the law or something equally proper, and if you'd actually been *seen* in what were called "dubious circumstances" it would never have been forgotten and it might affect the whole of your career. But at the same time the ambience of man-of-the-world sophistication had to surround you. Nothing proven, but just this coy suggestion of manly naughtiness that nobody could pin down to dates or locations. Waggish. And Maidenhead has been waggish ever since. Theatrical people started using it for weekends, and that gave it a reputation of real wickedness; but I think it's just remained waggish at bottom.'

The river has remained shingly at bottom too, but punts are rare nowadays. One of the boat proprietors told me: 'We've got punts of course, but there's very little call. Now and again you get an eccentric, like. I had one last year. He'd brought a girl with a picture hat and he was fussing round her like an old hen. "Masses of cushions, skipper," he told me. He was dressed a bit nostalgic himself—cream flannels with a faint pinstripe, and a Leander tie. And he'd brought an old-fashioned wind-up portable gramophone. He had records of Jack Smith, the Whispering Baritone, singing *Annabelle Lee* and that sort of thing. Sounded ever so thin over the water they did. But it was just like the old days. I remember all those when I was a kid. That's a rarity nowadays, though. If I let a punt out at all they get in a muddle with the pole half the time and I have to go and heave 'em away from the rushes or somewhere. Motor launches is what they want now. Change their minds each generation, they do. It was punts, then it was skiffs, then it was rowers, then it was outboards; now it's cabin cruisers and yachting caps to match. Change their minds to keep pace, they do. We've got to change with them, keep in business. Otherwise where'd you be? Well, we've got a good example : the old vicar did.'

There seem to have been several Vicars of Bray—which village is a mile south of Maidenhead, on the Berkshire bank —who lived through four or five reigns and turned their coats according to the religious colour prevailing. The first was Simon Alwyn, who switched to and from popery and protestantism to suit Henry the Eighth, Edward the Sixth, Mary Tudor, and Elizabeth the First. Later ones were Peter Pendleton, Simon Symons, and Francis Carswell, and all of them worshipped the okay god of the day. The vicar in the song (which was written by an officer of George the First's army) was an amalgam of all four and a send-up of the idea of the immutability of religious fervour. He keeps going through five stanzas and a reign is fitted to each—'In good King Charles's golden days', 'When Royal James possessed the crown,' 'When William was our king declared', 'When gracious Anne became our queen', and 'When George in pudding-time[1] came o'er'. Which of the actual vicars swore to keep his preferment regardless of the reigning monarch's faith is anybody's guess. They probably all did, knowing what was good for business and themselves.

The example of change to fit the times' conditions has been followed by others than boat proprietors and vicars. Restaurateurs at Bray have made plenty of hay in the sunshine of the expense account and the weekend tycoons' fervent longing for 'river tranquillity'—a phrase coined in the upper echelons of big business to express the kind of treatment needed by those

1. George the First was a fat man.

suffering from that curious malaise 'management fatigue'. Executives leaving London on Thursday afternoon for the weekend are said to be 'rolling from the rat-race to the river', and whether or not the rolling is done in a company-owned Rolls, Maidenhead or Bray are the likeliest objectives. There, pretentiously Snowcem'd cottages swap owners at inflated prices and table reservations are made at the Hind's Head in case the Queen should make one of her occasional visits.

Whether this stretch of the Thames has any tranquillising effects on management fatigue I don't know; but reproductions of Fred Walker's tranquil picture *The Harbour of Refuge*, depicting the Bray almshouses round a quadrangle of lawn, are sold in big numbers. Many of them, according to the man who sells them, end up on the walls of city offices and Mayfair pent-houses—'They like to take a breath of Bray back with them. Well, you can understand it with all those diesel fumes.' They also take back with them, and help to perpetuate, the fallacy that Monkey Island, just below Bray, is named for the jolly monkeys painted on the ceiling of the fishing lodge built there by the Duke of Marlborough. The name is in fact a corruption of Monk Eyot—an eyot, or ait, being a little island—and this particular eyot being one that was chucked like a bone at the monks fleeing from Bisham Abbey after the Dissolution—a consolation prize that carried fishing rights with it, and prevented the monks becoming a charge upon the new landowners. Marlborough's artist, a Frenchman, had less English than he liked to think, was confused by the look and sound of the words Monk Eyot, and went ahead and painted the monkeys. 'A pretty turn upon the words,' Marlborough said, combining gentlemanly consideration for the painter's feelings with contempt for monks, 'You are a subtle fellow.'

10

A Very Lordly Water

I

THE river at Windsor follows a serpentine course. There are islands large and small (the biggest one carries Windsor race course), S-bends, and backwaters in profusion. Nothing could be more appropriate than the curvaceous name Windleshores, which the place was originally called. The winding shores, though, had little to do with the selection of the site for the castle. The river here bisects a round chalk hill a hundred feet high, and it was this hill that determined the site. There could indeed not be a more obvious place for a fortress. It commands the river and the river crossing, and if the surveyor decided to build on the southern half of the hill the fortress would be further protected by forest. William the Conqueror did just this. He bought Windleshores from the manorial owners, the abbots of Westminster, the price being a similar number of hides of land in Essex, and began building the fortress almost before the battlefields of Hastings had been cleared.

By 1070 the walls were up, vestigial defences were in position, and William was in residence. He summoned his bishops to a synod later that year and told them that his fortress was as indestructible as the church. Thirty years later his son, Henry the First, destroyed it. But William could have meant his statement symbolically. It was in any case only a wooden fort—probably little more than a palisade. Henry extended the area of the fortifications to a dozen acres and his grandson,

Henry the Second, built again, this time in stone, in good time for *his* son, John, to be besieged there by the barons who were later to force him to fix his seal—he couldn't write—to Magna Carta—'Therefore it is our will and command that the English Church shall be free, and that men in our kingdom shall have and keep all these liberties, rights, and concessions, freely and quietly, fully and wholly, for themselves and their heirs, and us and our heirs, for ever'.

Magna Carta, Windsor Castle, and the Thames from Windsor down to Runnymede, where the charter was signed, have all been adopted by fervent chauvinists and phlegmatic liberals alike as symbols of the immutability of the British way of life. But in fact only Magna Carta—a piece of parchment twelve by twenty-six inches kept in the library of Salisbury Cathedral —remains unchanged in physical form. The castle has been reduced, enlarged, reconstructed, and restored by almost every monarch since William the Conqueror. You couldn't today find a trace of the original. The river has changed less but noticeably. The chalk hill on which Windsor is built rises from a bed of clay, and it is this clay, through which the river runs, which by its marshy nature has caused the changes of course, the pattern of islands, and the ancillary streams and backwaters. Some of its later changes accompanied some of the earlier changes in the castle—indeed were causally interlinked with them. As for example in the building of St George's Chapel.

There had been a chapel in the castle precincts certainly since the time of Edward the Third—five monarchs and a hundred years back—and probably much earlier, when Edward the Fourth commanded work to begin on 'a new church here by our home and castle, as great as that of Westminster'. He was in many ways a man of great imagination— he sponsored what was undoubtedly the greatest English event of the fifteenth century, the setting up of Caxton's printing press—and he must quickly have seen that any such huge church as that of Westminster, with its complex French design, would fit uneasily into the design of a stronghold that was essentially two baileys flanking a keep, the whole rising impressively from a cliff overhanging the river. The two would cancel each other out. He, or his master mason, therefore reconceived the original plan and reduced the scale. But the design was to be magnificent all the same—flying buttresses and a vaulted stone roof being two of its principal features.

Much of the stone for the church came down river from Gloucestershire. One chronicler said that 'the grete fletes of stone boats made quick the building of the Kings church at Windsor, the river being fast of flow in many seasons and bringing the stone so near to the masons at their work that no time was lost'. Fast of flow the river may have been; but, as I've shown, it also spilt treacherously over the land in many places, and hereabouts it was going through one of its metamorphoses—aided by several excessively wet winters—and had oozed marshily over the valley as far north as where Slough now is, and south well into Windsor Forest. Many of the barges bringing the stone got bogged down and sank with the great weight of their loads. The stone had to be dragged up year after year when the drier weather came and some primitive efforts at reclamation could be made. All this naturally delayed work on the chapel; and although that chronicler writes of the quick building it was in fact nearly a century before the work was near completion (this, admittedly, is quick by standards normally associated with the building of the churches of medieval days).

Even then the river continued to be a hinderance as well as a help; and in the end it was decided to scrap the idea of a stone roof because so much stone and time had been lost to the avaricious grip of the Bucks and Berks marshes. Oaks were hewn in the distant parts of Windsor Forest where the ground was higher and firmer and a timber roof built over the splendid edifice. By the time Henry the Seventh came to the throne, though (in 1485), the river had oozed its way back into a better defined bed, débris from the building up at the castle had been beaten into the boggy surrounds, and a much higher percentage of stone could be delivered to the site.

Henry called in carpenters and masons and got them to replace the timber roof with the vaulted stone one that had originally been planned by Edward. The marvellous fan vaulting was a triumph of the masons' art—and a triumph over the sodden opposition of the river, or so it must have seemed.

As things eventuated, however, it might have been wiser to keep the timber roof in spite of the magnificence of the stone one. The great weight proved to be too much for the fabric of the building and after the passage of a few more centuries the foundations were found to be sinking and major repairs had to be carried out. These weren't completed till 1930. 'Had the river had its way,' wrote Sir George Gilbert Scott, who was responsible for the Victorian murals, 'the Chapel of Saint George would be topped with beams and not with stone; and who knows but what Father Thames is wiser than us with all our learning.'

II

Across the river from Windsor is Eton College, founded by Henry the Sixth in 1440. Henry's life was bounded by the Thames. He was born at Windsor and was murdered while saying his prayers in the Tower of London. The last of the three kings of the house of Lancaster, he was much given to learning and piety. During the periods when he lost his reason as a consequence of an essentially pacific nature being forced to endure the ugly conflict of the Wars of the Roses, he is said to have been tranquillised by sitting by, or being rowed upon, the Thames and having someone speak pastoral verse softly into his ear :

> And the river that I sate upon
> It made such a noise as it ron,
> Accordaunt with the birdës armony
> Me thought it was the best melody
> That might ben heard of any mon.

The birdës armony and other characteristics of the bucolic have remained much in evidence ever since among writers who have viewed the prospect of Eton and Windsor from the river. As recently as 1929 the late Percy Lubbock was rhapsodising in *Shades of Eton* : 'The fortune of Eton is such that the place itself is all a paragon of noble style, and I don't speak only of the beauty of the ancient buildings, but also of the manner in which nature and history work together in the watery valley to dignify the life of the school. The river throws its arm about Eton with an ample swing. The Thames is a very lordly water, in these its middle reaches. Shy and shadowy in its younger course, by the time it comes within hail of the great pile of the Castle it has long lost its diffidence; it broadens and flashes in the noonday, sliding placidly, but with pride. The cool-haired nymphs of the Isis are left behind, in the devious retirement of the upper stream; or if any attend the progress of the grander flood, they lurk apart among the willows and reeds of the backwaters, where the swan and her cygnets find their haven. Through the middle of the sunlight and the bounty of the broad royal valley flows the Thames; and only the level streak of the kingfisher's flight is brilliant enough to be worn by the river, where the blaze of the day quenches all lesser glories. This is beauty noble and largehanded, beauty with authority and profusion, and Eton is half encircled in it. Consider what it gives us, that in our picture of the background of the school, and of the years that we spent in it, meanness of style isn't seen or thought of; it is swept over by our countless familiarity with the renown of this green stretch of the hollow land, the heart of England. And more than this, our place in the valley of the Thames has given us the sight of history— history that has flowed down our valley as steadily as the river itself, through the centuries of the life of the school. I think of the softness of mist and shade beneath the huge rampart of the Castle on its height : and then of the noble poise and outline of the vast mass itself, grey and dim in the morning freshness—that precipitous range of the Castle, lifted against the sky, which dominates all our Eton days; and with this there comes the sense of being face to face with the display of the fortunes of England, and our own domain, looped in the embrace of the Thames, is in contact with fate on a grand scale, with history that goes rolling past our border, down the broadening valley to London and the sea.'

This is lush writing indeed; but it fits a lush scene. It is the end of the stretch from Cliveden and the Thames recovers, briefly, from the pseudo-romanticism foisted upon it by the dire effects of Maidenhead and Bray. There is no doubt that, from the river, the castle is, as not only Lubbock, but also Defoe, said, 'the most beautiful and pleasantly situated Castle, and Royal Palace, in the whole Isle of Great Britain'. And on the fourth of June, when Eton's boating procession takes to the water, there are some pleasant genuinely romantic effects.

Beyond Windsor the river has had to cope, and no doubt will continue to cope, with other burdens than pseudo-romanticism. To my way of thinking, one of the most melancholy of those burdens was the disguised boat in which the decapitated body of Charles the First was secretly borne down from London on a bitter day in February, 1649, watched over by his friend and bishop, William Juxon. Since early in January the Thames had been frozen over in London, and John Evelyn writes of the 'bitter tempests of winds'. The boat encountered ice floes at Chertsey and was poled off them by fishermen. It was challenged at Datchet by Parliamentarians. But these further icy obstacles were also evaded, and in flurries of snow the secret hearse moored at Windsor and the coffin was borne up to the castle. Burial rites were forbidden by Cromwell's parliament, and the committal to the tomb beneath the choir of St George's Chapel had to be silent. 'It was truly a silence of the tomb', Juxton wrote, 'in which our excellent king left my hand.'

An Eye on the River

I

MUSING on the melancholy silence of 'the fair and fatal
king' I left Windsor and was soon musing on the fact that
from here on silence becomes less and less a characteristic of
the Thames. The sounds of high-road traffic, lawn mowers,
and recreation grounds shudder over the flat terrain. It's like
listening to London through the narrow end of a funnel. Cecil
Day Lewis wrote :

> You that love England, that have an ear for her music,
> The slow movement of clouds in benediction :
> Clear arias of light thrilling over her uplands,
> Over the chords of summer sustained peacefully;
> Ceaseless the leaves' counterpoint in a west wind lively,
> Blossom and river rippling loveliest allegro,
> And the storms of wood, strings, brass at year's finale :
> Listen, can you not hear the entrance of a new theme?

The new theme he was writing about was the theme of war;
but his final line serves me perfectly in my own context. The
theme of London may be screened by the squeaks and per-
golas of suburbia, but nevertheless it enters audibly and visibly
here. Counties mix like the dissolves in one of those travelogue
films with breezy dialogue—'Here at Coopers Hill a hundred
miles of pastoral Berkshire give way to Surrey's bungalows
and bustling humour; over the river at Wraysbury is Anker-

wyke House, where Henry Eight—the old so-and-so!—stole
a kiss from Anne Boleyn under the yew tree; and it's still
Bucks—but not for long, for the country ditch muscles in from
the north and beyond it are the great reservoirs of Staines—
the Metropolitan Water Board's tribute to the people of
London—and we're in Middlesex.' I could almost hear the
chatty voice, and I could certainly see the Wraysbury Gravel
Company's excavations, the varnish works, the gas works, car
parks, and other signs of metropolitan takeover.

There is, too, a feeling of historical, as well as regional,
metathesis. At Runnymede, on Magna Carta Island, the
National Trust takes care of national history (and national
character) with suitable notices, the first of which reads: 'In
these meads on 15th June 1215, King John, at the instance of
deputies from the whole community of the realm, granted the
Great Charter, the earliest of constitutional documents, where-
under ancient and cherished customs were confirmed and
abuses redressed, the administration of justice facilitated, new
provisions formulated for the peace, and every individual per-
petually secured in the free enjoyment of his life and property.'
The other notice reads: 'Boating parties forbidden to land.'
These are the trumpetings of a national oracle. But after
Runnymede history debouches, like the river, on the capital.
It becomes the history of London, of a nation within a nation.

II

So far as the Thames is concerned, London begins at Teddington. Just below the weir there is a boundary stone marking
the administrative change from the Thames Conservancy
board to the Port of London Authority. Kipling perpetuated a
popular fallacy in writing that Teddington meant 'tide end
town'; but it doesn't: it means 'land of the sons of Tedda'.
All the same, the tidal waters do end here, and if you sniff
hard enough and other smells don't get in the way you can
smell the salt in the air. The other smells likely to overpower

the salt are of effluent, smoke, diesel oil, petrol, fish, and detergents—the London pomander. Though possibly less of an olfactory gallimaufry in earlier days, the smell of London has often wafted up and down the river in strong concentrations.

It was, for example, unsuitably malodorous on that night in May 1471, when the body of the murdered Henry the Sixth was brought up river from the Tower by the monks of Chertsey for transitory interment in their abbey before being entombed at Windsor. The cortège of boats was lit by torches and the monks ceaselessly chanted the funeral dirges until they came within sound of the abbey bell tolling. The smell of the torches of burning tar was overcome by the stink of London's sewage, which was borne on a following wind, and the monks' clerk recorded that 'a smel ther was as grete as deth, but for no berien [burial] was it mäd'. Smells are indeed not made for burial, and if they are troublesome the only cure is to abort them before they grow too big. This wasn't easily done in the fifteenth century because London's sewage ran through the streets and open gutters and ditches. True, much of it found its way into the Thames and would be to some extent neutralised there by the water. But there was no way of coping with the foulness of the streets. The only relief from bad smells in those days was for sweet smelling flowers to be tossed in the path of those whom it would be insulting to offend, and indeed this was done for kings and others of the upper crust. But it could hardly be effective on a river journey with breezes blowing; and in any case monks were used to all kinds of mortifications of the flesh, the dead king wouldn't have cared, and the clerk was reporting rather than complaining.

Later, when a more efficient sewerage disposal system was invented it took the effluent by covered ways into the river, which in time became overburdened with it to the extent of becoming excessively de-oxygenised (as I explained on p. 133) and the stink of pollution rose off the water itself. Complaints then became loud and insistent.

The people of Chelsea told the Lords and Commons in an 1827 petition, 'That the water taken up from the river Thames at Chelsea for the use of the inhabitants of the western portion of the Metropolis being charged with the contents of the great common sewers, the drainings from dunghills and laystalls, the refuse of hospitals, slaughterhouses, colour, lead, and soap works, drug-mills, and manufactories, and with all sorts of decomposed animal and vegetable substances, rendering the said water offensive and destructive to health, ought no longer to be taken up, by any of the water companies, from so foul a source'.

These petitioners were complaining specifically about the unhealthy quality of the water for drinking, and indeed the Metropolis Water Act of 1852, which came about as a result of the Royal Commission appointed in response to the petition, makes it illegal to supply drinking water from the tidal part of the Thames. But there were plenty who complained about the smells as well as about the quality of the water, and their cause was taken up by a nauseated press.

'Effluvia of this nature', the *Morning Post* said sternly, 'are doing more harm to the Capital than an army of Radicals could do in a dozen lifetimes. Only in such remote villages as the Heights of Hampstead is one truly freed intire from the assault on the olfactory senses. The men of business who must perforce work in the City are assailed at every change of breeze with effluvia from the foetid reaches of Barking and Greenwich. The Holland eels inhabiting the river can no longer bear the stench and have returned to their own purer shores; and the deposits of filth that lie upon the banks of the Thames at low tide add, if that were possible, to the pervading disgust. The matter of the purity of the water supply may have been settled by the Gentlemen of the House; but they should now turn their attention to the purity of the air—Nay! they have no need to *turn* their attention : if they will but take their kerchiefs from their noses the impurity will be made manifest.'

Parliament of course needed to be prodded into action even though the river washed the doorsteps of the House and the smell on hot dry days wafted into the chamber. But the right kind of action was not easy to decide. Cesspools had been abolished in 1848 and more and more houses were being fitted with water closets; more and more industrial plants were discharging more and more of their waste products into the river; and the mud and muck were being increasingly stirred up by the paddles and screws of steamships. Parliament could, and did, pass an Act forcing the Metropolitan Water Board to complete, by the end of 1860, whatever works the Board might think necessary 'for preventing all or any part of the sewage within the metropolis from flowing or passing into the river Thames in or near the metrolpolis', but this in effect was no more than a passing of buck, for 'whatever works the Board might think necessary' might easily turn out to result in no works at all.

However, the Board was conscientious enough to take the matter very seriously, and told its chief engineer, Joseph Bazalgette, to produce a scheme. The scheme was duly produced. It recommended that the sewage should be diverted from outfalls higher up the river than Barking—twelve miles from London Bridge—and released into the river only on ebb tides and where the average volume of tidal water was four hundred times greater than the volume of sewage released into it. It also recommended 'the construction of terrace embankments on both sides of the Thames to confine the tidal channel, accelerate the velocity of the stream, and prevent the exposure of the bed and banks of the river'. The scheme was discussed and juggled with, put in hand, and eventually completed by 1875.

As might have been expected, the volume of sewage kept pace with the works and by the time the outfall at Barking was completed the dilution ration was considerably less than four hundred to one. The residents of central London subdued their complaints to a mere whisper, but the residents of Barking raised theirs to a shout. There were more investigations, more Royal Commissions, more suggestions—and, of course, a continually increasing stench. Works for the precipitation of the sewage—that is, its separation into solids and liquids by chemical means—were constructed and these helped for the time being. But stripped to its nub the problem was the one of increasing population and industrialisation. And this has remained the problem to the present day.

1934 and 1935 brought renewed shrieks of protest against the foulness of the river and 1949 brought synthetic detergents, which created more trouble, for they have the effect of further reducing the rate at which water is able to dissolve oxygen from the air. The result of all this—apart from the smell—was the establishment of a Water Pollution Research Laboratory and the appointment of a Thames Survey Committee and a Departmental Committee (it was a department of the Ministry of Housing and Local Government) on the effects of Heated and Other Effluents and Discharges on the Condition of the Tidal Reaches of the River Thames. That was in 1951. The Committee presented its report in 1961. Three years later, under the aegis of the Department of Scientific and Industrial Research, the Thames Survey Committee and the Water Pollution Research Laboratory presented *their* reports. In book form they ran to six hundred and nine pages of large size and weighed fifteen pounds.

These reports were supplemented by twenty-six studies of particular aspects of the problem, all written by specialists and bearing such titles as *Corrosion of Ships' Propellers in Polluted Estuaries, The Regimen of the Thames Estuary as Affected by Current, Salinities, and River Flow, The Evolution of Gas from the Bottom Deposits of the Estuary,* and *The Ultimate Oxygen Demand and Course of Oxidation of Sewage Effluents.* No-one, in fact, could say that the problem had not had proper attention. But although recommendations were made and action planned as a result of the recommendations, it will be a long time before the pollution problem is satisfactorily solved. Meanwhile, the London pomander still includes among its constituent smells the smell of the polluted Thames. It would not be true to say that Londoners walk beside or across their river continually holding handkerchiefs to their noses; but there are many times when stiff breezes bring the stink of the estuary reaches as well as the salt of the North Sea.

London is built in a hollow between rising plateaux of heavy clay. These plateaux stretch up to the heights of Hampstead in the north and to Forest Hill in the south. Geologically, this hollow feature is called a flood plain. The stormwater off both northern and southern hills drains into the plain and into the river and there are records galore of the times the plain has been flooded in fact as well as name.

The historian Stow says that 'In the year 1236 the River of Thames overflowing to the banks, caused the marshes about Woolwitch to be all on a sea, wherein boats and other vessels were carried with the stream; so that besides cattle, the greatest number of men, women and children, inhabitants there, were drowned: and in the great Palace of Westminster men did row with wherries in the midst of the Hall, being forced to ride to their chambers. Moreover, in the year 1242, the Thames overflowing the banks about Lambhithe, drowned houses and fields by the space of six miles, so that in the great hall at Westminster men took their horses, because the water ran over all.'

Pepys wrote on 7th December 1663, 'I hear that there was last night the greatest tide that ever was remembered in England to have been in this river; all Whitehall having been drowned'. In 1922 there were floods that made the river rise to the top of the parapet of Victoria Embankment. And during the night of 6th–7th January 1928 there was a storm in the North Sea that caused a tidal backwash that raised the Thames to its highest recorded level. Fourteen people were drowned in that flood. One of them was a waiter who worked at the Café Royal, and I managed to track down his widow. Her story will be the last stroke of this profile because it seems to me to be particularly fitted to complete it. Here, I mean talk of one disaster to lead to talk of another. But this one was not a disaster of flood or any other meteorological disturbance. It was a disaster caused by that other engine of destruction, human fallibility.

IV

Two of the steamship paddles that stirred up the mucky sludge on the bed of the river and added to the effluential stench in Victorian days were those of the *Princess Alice*, a pleasure boat belonging to the London Steamboat Company and built on lines very similar to those of the Salter steamer I came down from Oxford in—though that one, of course, had propellers, not paddles. The *Princess Alice* was without flounces of respectability : she had been named after the Grand Duchess of Hesse-Darmstadt, one of Queen Victoria's daughters; and she was referred to by her owners as 'the Shah's boat' because she had once carried the Shah of Persia and his entourage on an official visit to Greenwich. But she was a working boat for all that, and from spring to autumn she steamed up and down the river from London Bridge to Shoeburyness, a distance of forty-five miles and about as far as you can go without actually venturing out from the Thames into the North Sea. There were stops *en route* and passengers could be picked up or set down at any of them, buying tickets for the distances they wanted to travel, as with a train or bus. This made it impossible to tell how many people were aboard at any particular time, but the ship could easily carry a thousand passengers.

When she set off on the morning of Saturday, 3rd September 1878 there were about five hundred aboard. During the trip the number increased, and on the return journey there were about eight hundred aboard just after 7.30 p.m. when she was in Galleons Reach, a stretch of the river between Woolwich and Barking—and near, incidentally, the newly constructed sewage outfall that the people of Barking were becoming vociferous about. The width of the river there is over six hundred yards even at low tide, so there is plenty of room to manœuvre even quite big vessels, and the *Princess Alice* was no liner in size (she was seventy-three yards long, less than an eighth of the width of the river).

There is a rule of the river just as there is a rule of the road : ships keep to the right and when going in opposite directions pass each other port to port—that is, left side to left side—and all ships carry red and green lights after dark to indicate their port and starboard sides. However, though the rule is to keep a starboard course it needs to be flexibly interpreted because ships in rivers often need to cross from side to side of the waterway to avoid obstructions or take advantage of variations in the tide, which runs slower at the banks than in the middle of the stream. So in certain circumstances it would be perfectly sound navigation for two ships to ignore the rule and pass starboard to starboard. But helmsmen clearly need a set of subsidiary rules to guide them according to the circumstances; and a rough and ready mnemonic in doggerel form was in general use at the time :

Two steam ships passing

Green to green or red to red
Perfect safety—go ahead.

Two steam ships meeting

When all three lights I see ahead
I port my helm and show my red.

Two steam ships crossing

If to my starboard red appear
It is my duty to keep clear;
Act as judgement says is proper
Port—or starboard—back—or stop her.

But when upon my port is seen
A steamer's starboard light of green,
For me there's nought to do or see
That green to port keeps clear of me.

All ships must keep a good lookout

Both in safety and in doubt
I always keep a good lookout;
In danger, with no room to turn,
I ease her, stop her, go astern.

The verses were evidently ignored, though, by someone on this particular night. There was another ship called the *Bywell Castle* coming downstream at the time (it was dark, the sun having set about an hour previously) and the two ships collided—with terrible results for the *Princess Alice,* which was struck amidships, just forward of the starboard paddlebox, and sank to the bottom of the river within four minutes.

Of the eight hundred people aboard, six hundred were drowned, and others died later from shock, pneumonia, and the effects of swallowing the poisonous water of the Thames. But there were also some miraculous survivals, and some phlegmatic ones—including a Mr Henry Read and his wife, proprietors of a stationery shop in Oxford Street, who told a reporter that they arrived home at 11 o'clock, 'rather earlier than we had expected'.

The sinking of the *Princess Alice* seems to have been the greatest disaster in the long history of the Thames: indeed, I couldn't find anything to equal it, in terms of lives lost, in the history of Britain, except of course as a consequence of war. There was an inquest at which much conflicting evidence was given. Some of it suggested that the captain of the *Princess Alice* was, or earlier had been, drunk; but he wasn't alive to answer this accusation and in any case wasn't at the helm at the time. There seems also to have been much confusion in the minds of the two helmsmen about which way to turn when they saw each other's ships approaching.

The coroner, a Mr Charles Joseph Cartter, shows signs of having been far from impartial and of misdirecting the jury, whose verdict was, 'That the death of the said William Beachey[1] was occasioned by drowning in the waters of the River Thames from a collision that occurred after sunset between a steam vessel called the *Bywell Castle* and a steam vessel called the *Princess Alice,* whereby the *Princess Alice* was cut in two and sank, such collision not being wilful; that the *Bywell Castle* did not take the necessary precaution of easing, stopping, and reversing her engines in time and that the *Princess Alice* contributed to the collision by not stopping and going astern; that all collisions in the opinion of the jury might in future be avoided if proper and stringent rules and regulations were laid down for all steam navigation on the River Thames'.

When, subsequently, there was a Board of Trade inquiry the conclusion reached was that the *Princess Alice* was to blame because her helmsman acted 'in default of the . . . rule [the port-to-port rule] and the collision was unavoidable by the *Bywell Castle*'. Which of these assemblies of gentlemen was right no-one can now say; and the transcripts of evidence given at both the inquest and the court of inquiry, though voluminous, show that there was really very little to help them establish more than that the collision was caused by human fallibility. And human fallibility had its grim memorial in the observation of the diver who was sent down to examine the wreck. 'The cabins,' he said, 'were full of bodies standing erect and all packed together at the exits.'

---

1. Beachey's body was the first to be recovered from the river, so he was, as it were, the representative subject of the inquest. Many of the corpses remained unidentified.

V

During the days following the *Princess Alice* disaster, when bodies were being recovered from the river and taken to commandeered warehouses nearby for grisly exhibition and identification, a man made a great nuisance of himself by parading up and down the river banks and into and out of the proxy mortuaries carrying a placard on which was written: 'CAN WE BE MASTERS OF THE SEA IF WE CANNOT KEEP A PLEASURE BOAT AFLOAT ON THE THAMES? THE RIVER HAS HAD HER REVENGE.' He was continually moved on by policemen, but since he was doing no actual harm he couldn't be arrested. Besides, he was well known as a local character and, when he wasn't playing the part of an exasperated cynic and breaking in on mourners' private distress, he was regarded with some affection. His name was Douglas Chellow, and he had been born eighty-eight years earlier in High Timber Street, Rotherhithe.

Since his birth Chellow had never been outside London and only very rarely outside the area bounded on the west by Chelsea, on the east by Southend, and on the north and south by the streets immediately flanking the Thames. He says of himself, in a series of autobiographical broadsheets he printed when the fancy took him, that he 'had some education'; and indeed this must be true, for at different times he was a printer, a publisher, an historian, and a clerk. But most of his life was spent beachcombing, assembling information about the Thames, and retailing it in written or verbal form to anyone he could persuade to attend to him. One such interested party was Charles Whitehead, the writer who introduced Dickens to the publishers Chapman and Hall and by doing so brought about the commission for *The Pickwick Papers*. Whitehead says that he encountered Chellow during a stroll near Blackfriars Bridge.

'He was a most curious fellow, mumbling to himself one minute and shouting to the chimney-pots the next. He wrung his hands as if finding all hopeless, then suddenly quietened and was all smiles and concern. It seemed that he wanted only to convey his love of the river to anyone who would listen and I found the interest to hear him many times. He was truly a fine guide and seemed to have dates and clear descriptions in his mind. His method, if you were interested, was to take you by the hand and lead you to Blackfriars or Westminster or London Bridge, where a purview of the Thames might be obtained, and lead forth on a lecture that would continue till you were surfeited. His command of facts seemed to be remarkable, and from notes I made during and after his recitals I can assemble one of his *little lectures* almost as he might give it, though to capture the tone of his voice and the manner of his delivery is impossible. Enow, I remind myself, that his gestures were *large*, like those of a Thespian trying his art upon the board, and his voice rich and various. According to mood he might take it upon himself to take a period of historical occurrence; but totted up into a sum one would be thus presented with a History in Miniature :

' "Romans, Saxons, and Danes all were here before the Conqueror. All trod London bridge before us, all gazed into this the noblest of rivers. Franks, Flemings, Germans and Hollanders have brought their ships. Arabians have sent their gold, Sabeans their frankincense and spice, Scythians their arms of war, Babylonians their oil, the Seres their stones and raiment, the northern lands their sables.

' "There where Bermondsey lies were once the hostelries of monks; Saint Olave's you see in Tooley Street was there before the Normans came; Gundulf of Rochester built William's keep, the Tower, upon the Roman wall, and no foe has passed its bastion these eight hundred years.

' "By Rotherhithe where I was born, London's fleet was built at the orders of the Black Prince, and sailed from there to France. Chaucer lived in Aldgate. John Philpot sailed against Mercer the Scot, caught and hanged him, and was made mayor. Down at Canvey, Wat Tyler and Jack Cade both plotted rebellion. And on this bridge one Saint George's day Lindsay of Glenesk met Willes of London in joust.

' "Lord Mayor's procession was held first upon the river" —here he seized upon his listener's arm and earnestly entreated him to imagine such a splendid sight, though I recall it well myself—"for there were then no Law Courts and the King's judges made their judgements at Westminster. So it came about that Sir John Norman, mayor of that year,[1] built a barge and sailed in it to the royal palace to be sworn in and the liverymen followed his example and themselves built boats to follow him...'

At this point Whitehead either stopped listening or lost his notes, for one hears no more of Chellow through him. But Chellow himself wrote, among many other things, a worthwhile account of the great frost of 1814 and printed and sold it in broadsheet form as one of his self-imposed activities as a guide to, and amateur historian of, the Thames. He wrote:

'On Sunday, the 30th of January, the immense masses of ice that floated from the upper parts of the river, in consequence of the thaw on the two preceding days, blocked up the Thames between Blackfriars and London Bridges; and afforded every probability of its being frozen over in a day or two. Some adventurous persons even now walked on different parts, and on the next day, Monday the 31st, the expectation was realised. During the whole of the afternoon, hundreds of people were assembled on Blackfriars and London Bridges, to see people cross and recross the Thames on the ice. At one time seventy persons were counted walking from Queenhithe to the opposite shore. The frost of Sunday night so united the vast mass to render it immovable by the tide.

'On Tuesday, February 1, the river presented a thoroughly solid surface over that part which extends from Blackfriars Bridge to some distance below Three Crane Stairs, at the

1. In spite of Whitehead's assurance of Chellow's knowledge of dates, he doesn't quote any, Norman was mayor in 1453 and the procession of boats remained a feature of the ceremony until 1857.

bottom of Queen Street, Cheapside. The watermen placed notices at the end of all streets leading to the city side of the river, announcing a safe footway over, which attracted immense crowds, and in a short time thousands perambulated the rugged plain, where a variety of amusements were provided. Among the more curious of these was the ceremony of roasting a small sheep, or rather toasting or burning it over a coal fire, placed in a large iron pan. For a view of this extraordinary spectacle sixpence was demanded, and willingly paid. The delicate meat, when *done*, was sold at a shilling a slice and termed *Lapland Mutton*.

'There were a great number of booths ornamented with streamers, flags, and signs, and within them there was a plentiful store of favourite luxuries with most of the multitude, *gin, beer*, and *ginger-bread*. The thoroughfare opposite Three Crane Stairs was complete and well frequented. It was strewn with ashes, and afforded a very safe, although a very rough path. Near Blackfriars Bridge, however, the way was not equally severe; a plumber, named *Davis,* having imprudently ventured to cross with some lead in his hands, sank between two masses of ice, and rose no more. Two young women nearly shared a similar fate; they were rescued from their perilous situation by the prompt efforts of two watermen. Many a fair nymph indeed was embraced in the *icy arms* of old Father Thames;—three young Quakeresses had a sort of semi-bathing, near London Bridge, and when landed on terra-firma made the best of their way through the Borough, amidst the shouts of an admiring populace. From the entire obstruction the tide did not appear to ebb for some days more than one half the usual mark.

'On Wednesday, Feb 2, the sports were repeated, and the Thames presented a complete FROST FAIR. The grand *mall* or walk now extended from Blackfriars Bridge to London Bridge; this was named the *City road*, and was lined on each side with persons of all descriptions. Eight or ten printing presses were erected and numerous pieces commemorative of the great frost were printed on the ice. Some of these frosty typographers displayed considerable taste in their specimens. At one of the presses, an orange-coloured standard was hoisted with the watch-word ORANGE BOVEN in large characters. This was an allusion to the recent restoration of the Stadt-holder to the government of Holland, which had been for several years under the dominion of the French. From this press the following papers were issued.

' "Amidst the arts which on the THAMES appear,
    To tell the wonders of this *icy* year,
    PRINTING claims prior place, which at one view
    Erects a monument of THAT and YOU."

'*Another* :

' "You that walk here, and do design to tell
    Your children's children what this year befell,
    Come, buy this print, and it will then be seen,
    That such a year as this has seldom been."

'Another of these *stainers of paper* addressed the spectators in the following terms : "Friends, now is your time to support the freedom of the press. Can the press have greater liberty? here you find it working in the middle of the Thames; and if you encourage us by buying our impressions, we will keep it going in the true spirit of liberty during the frost." One of the articles printed and sold contained the following lines :

    Behold, the river Thames is frozen o'er,
    Which lately ships of mighty burden bore;
    Now different arts and pastimes here you see,
    But printing claims the superiority."

'The Lord's prayer and several other pieces were issued from these icy printing offices, and bought with the greatest avidity.
'On Thursday, Feb. 3, the number of adventurers increased.

Swings, bookstalls, dancing in a barge, suttling-booths,[1] play-ing at skittles, and almost every appendage of a fair on land, appeared now on the Thames. Thousands flocked to this sing-ular spectacle of sports and pastimes. The ice seemed to be a solid rock, and presented a truly picturesque appearance. The view of St Paul's and of the city with the white foreground had a very singular effect;—in many parts, the mountains of ice upheaved resembled the rude interior of a stone quarry.

'Friday, Feb 4. Each day brought a fresh accession of ped-lars to sell their wares; and the greatest rubbish of all sorts was raked up and sold at double and treble the original cost. Books and toys labelled *bought on the Thames* were in pro-fusion. The watermen profited exceedingly, for each person paid a toll of twopence or threepence before he was admitted to *Frost Fair*; some douceur was expected on the return. Some of them were said to have taken six pounds each in the course of a day.

'This afternoon, about five o'clock, three persons, an old man and two lads, were on a piece of ice above London Bridge, which suddenly detached itself from the main body, and was carried by the tide through one of the arches. They laid them-selves down for safety, and the boatmen at Billingsgate, put off to their assistance, and rescued them from their impending danger. One of them was able to walk, but the other two were carried, in a state of insensibility, to a public house, where they received every attention their situation required.

'Many persons were on the ice till late at night, and the effect by *moonlight* was singularly novel and beautiful. The bosom of the Thames seemed to rival the frozen climes of the north.

'Saturday, Feb. 5. This morning augured unfavourably for the continuance of FROST FAIR. The wind had veered to the south, and there was a light fall of snow. The visitors, however, were not to be deterred by trifles. Thousands again ventured, and there was still much life and bustle on the frozen element; the footpath in the centre of the river was hard and

1. A Georgian version of the caféteria

secure, and among the pedestrians were four donkeys; they trotted a nimble pace and produced considerable merriment. At every glance, there was a novelty of some kind or other. Gaming was carried on in all its branches. Many of the itinerant admirers of the profits gained by *E. O.*[1] *Tables, Rouge et Noir, Te-totum*, wheel of fortune, the garter &c. were industrious in their avocations, and some of their customers left the lures without a penny to pay the passage over a plank to the shore. Skittles was played by several parties, and the drinking tents were filled by females and their companions, dancing reels to the sound of fiddles, while others sat round large fires, drinking rum, grog, and other spirits. Tea, coffee, and eatables, were provided in abundance, and passengers were invited to eat by way of recording their visit. Several tradesmen, who at other times were deemed respectable, attended with their wares, and sold books, toys, and trinkets of almost every description.

'Towards the evening, the concourse thinned; rain began to fall, and the ice to crack, and on a sudden it floated with the printing presses, booths and merrymakers, to the no small dismay of publicans, typographers, shopkeepers, and sojourners.

'A short time previous to the general dissolution, a person near one of the printing presses, handed the following *jeu d'esprit* to its conductor; requesting that it might be printed on the Thames:

' "To Madam Tabitha Thaw. Dear dissolving dame, FATHER FROST and SISTER SNOW have boneyed my borders, formed an *idol of ice* upon my bosom, and all the LADS OF LONDON come to make merry: now as you love mischief, treat the multitude with a few cracks by a sudden visit, and obtain the prayers of the poor upon both banks. *Given at my own press,* the 5th Feb, 1814. THOMAS THAMES."

'The thaw advanced more rapidly than indiscretion and

1. Even-odd, a game similar to roulette.

heedlessness retreated. Two genteel-looking young men ventured on the ice above Westminster Bridge, notwithstanding the warnings of the watermen. A large mass on which they stood, and which had been loosened by the flood tide, gave way, and they floated down the stream. As they passed under Westminster Bridge they cried piteously for help. They had not gone far before they sat down, near the edge; this overbalanced the mass, they were precipitated into the flood, and overwhelmed for ever.

'A publican named Lawrence, of the Feathers, in Queenhithe, erected a booth on the Thames opposite Brook's Wharf, for the accommodation of the curious. At nine at night he left it in the care of two men, taking away all the liquors, except some gin, which he gave them for their own use.

'Sunday, Feb. 6. At two o'clock this morning, the tide began to flow with great rapidity at London Bridge; the thaw assisted the efforts of the tide, and the booth last mentioned was violently hurried towards Blackfriars Bridge. There were nine men in it, but in their alarm they neglected the fire and candles, which communicating with the covering, set it in a flame. They succeeded in getting into a lighter which had broken from its moorings. In this vessel they were wrecked, for it was dashed to pieces against one of the piers of Blackfriars Bridge: seven of them got on the pier and were taken off safely; the other two got into a barge while passing Puddle Dock.

'On this day, the Thames towards high tide (about 3 p.m.) presented a miniature idea of the Frozen Ocean; the masses of ice floating along, added to the great height of the water, formed a striking scene for contemplation. Thousands of disappointed persons thronged the banks; and many a 'prentice, and servant maid, sighed unutterable things at the sudden and unlooked-for destruction of FROST FAIR.

'Monday, Feb. 7. Immense fragments of ice yet floated, and numerous lighters, broken from their moorings, drifted in different parts of the river; many of them were complete wrecks. The frozen element soon attained its wonted fluidity,

and old Father Thames looked as cheerful and as busy as
ever.'

Chellow published this broadsheet in 1861, so he was presumably relying on notes made at the time or on memory.
Whichever it was his description is lively and shows no sign
of the eccentricity that overcame him later and resulted in his
ranting and raving against the authorities' 'neglect', as he
called it, of the river. They didn't neglect it, but they didn't
worship it either, in the sense that Chellow did, for in his last
months he built himself a hovel down on the bank at Greenwich reach and there, every morning, made worshipful obeisances like a Druid priest—throwing up his arms and then
prostrating himself on the shore and calling on London's river
to claim him as a follower—which the river one morning
conveniently did, for his body was revealed on the bank at low
tide.

VI

The cheerfulness of the Thames is often in doubt. Few things
look less cheerful than a river prickled with drenching rain.
But no-one can ever have been in doubt about its busyness
at the London end. Chellow certainly wasn't. Beside being
guide, philosopher, and friend to his favourite river he was
also its statistician—in a somewhat eccentric way, true, but
nonetheless assiduously. When a Mr P. Colquhoun, LL.D,
published, in 1800, an enormous *Treatise on the Commerce
and Police of the River Thames*, he can have little realised
what an ardent reader he was to find in Chellow. But ardent
Chellow certainly was, and when in 1815 he set up his first
printing shop—inspired, perhaps, by all that composition he'd
seen going on at the Frost Fair—he started with a press and
type he bought from the printer of Mr Colquhoun's book,
who presumably saw no harm in the setting up of an establishment rival to his own.

Colquhoun's book described itself at a length that was practically a book in itself: 'Containing an historical view of the

o

trade of the port of London; and suggesting means for preventing the depredations thereon, by a legislative system of
River Police. With an account of the functions of the various
magistrates and corporations exercising jurisdiction on the
river; and a general view of the penal and remediable statutes
connected with the subject.' And it rumbled away tirelessly
about how the river police, which had been established in 1798,
should be helped by the framing of new laws that would help
to prevent the depredations that were robbing the commerce
of London of ten million pounds a year, and adequately pun-
ish the mudlarks, scuffle-hunters, bumboatmen, watermen, rat-
catchers, and other workers on the river who were caught
with their fingers in the cargoes and warehouses. Deportation
and death were among the punishments for river thefts ordered
by various Acts of George the Second's reign, but river workers
had organised themselves and their rackets into such a state
of efficiency that magistrates could rarely break the chains of
evidence they produced to cover each other when caught.
And when they managed to impose fines for minor offences
the fines were paid from a general fund amassed by the workers
themselves as an insurance.

The river robbery racket had developed from an earlier—
and continuing—racket of piracy and smuggling, and was
highly successful because there was no adequate supervision
during the loading and unloading of ships and pilferage was
possible by many means—from blatantly open stealing to
devious ways of 'sampling' goods that were legal but left the
road open for wholesale plundering. Both the Crown and the
shipping companies were the losers, but it was a shipping company—specifically the West India—that established 'marine
police' who were backed by authority and were given the
opportunity of breaking the grip of the racketeers. And once
the marine police were into their stride Chellow took it upon
himself to analyse bills of lading and all the other impedimenta
of shipping administration and produce immensely complex
statistical charts which he headed 'Crimes against the River

Thames' and which he printed himself and sold for a few coppers if he could press people to buy them and gave away if he couldn't.

By this activity he clearly was demonstrating that he took river crimes as a personal affront against the river rather than against the unfortunate shipping companies. His eccentric enthusiasm may have been misplaced, but it couldn't have been exceeded; and Colquhoun himself, who met Chellow several times, said that 'if ever impediment be removed to the creation of a Society undeviating in its knowledge of, and affection for, the Thames river, and to prosecute all designs that promise to favour the river in every aspect, *Douglas Chellow* should be the very *Captain* thereof. For, as I see, he lives nothing but the Thames, has its soundings and tides in his head, knows every pint of its content, belabours those who subdue or belittle it with remarks betraying their ignorance, sees all of its unpleasing aspects as *advantages* to be whispered over like religious devotions, and will hear nought against it in any manner or form'.

No such society as Colquhoun had in mind came into being until 1962; but if Chellow had been alive then he would surely have been its President. This River Thames Society concerns itself with everything from the rights of way along footpaths near the river to proposing tremendous schemes for damming and barraging that would narrow the waterway and enable two main highways to be built alongside it. The Society is, in fact, a collective version of all Chellow's enthusiasms and eccentricities dispersed among its members. For example, at its first annual conference in 1963 it discussed, *inter alia*, river accidents and water safety, the trade and commerce of the river, and the problems of riverside local authorities in respect to planning. For two days an impressive collection of figures relating to shipping, tonnages, quantities of mud and sewage, amounts of water flowing to and fro, percentages of sewage effluent, and the number of people drowned in inland waters, were presented to an audience of members of the Society and delegates from bodies as widely varied as the Pure Rivers

Society (another organisation Chellow would surely have belonged to) and the National Association of Parish Councils.

One of the dignitaries addressing the conference referred to the aim that the Society is pledged to uphold—'preserving the character and soul of the great river which we all love'. This is the sort of thing dignitaries say when addressing conferences. Such phrases are a combination of oratorical fancy and sincerity and can be effective when imbued with the personality of the speaker. Flat on the paper they look, indeed, flat, and when analysed pose many questions. What is the 'soul' of a river, for instance? And surely there must be many people who are embodiments of the aphorism that without hate there cannot be love? An individual rather than a Society seemed to me the best bet for an epitome of what the Thames can mean.

VII

Mrs Louisa Rockett (as I shall call her), a stubby woman of sixty-six with heavy legs and arms and hair the colour of old string, lives in E.14. There is no need to locate her more narrowly than that. Like Chellow, she has lived by the river all her life, though she's been out of London from time to time, to visit relations in Macclesfield and Bristol, and once she travelled to Edinburgh because someone had told her it was the finest northern city—a statement with which she said, sensibly, that she 'couldn't neither agree nor disagree, not having seen none of the others.'

Her home is on the fifth floor of a modern block that was built to replace slummy cottages that were bombed during World War Two, when the Germans were aiming for the docks. Outside her front door a stone balcony runs the length of the block, and from it you can see an omega-shaped stretch of the Thames divided nomenclaturely into Limehouse Reach, Greenwich Reach, and Blackwall Reach, with the Lower Pool on the western extremity and Bugsby's Reach on the eastern. Embraced in the hollow of the omega are West India, Millwall,

and Railway Docks, and the Blackwall Basin, a tidal inlet
from the river connected directly with two of the West India
Docks and Railway Dock. In the days when Mrs Rockett
lived in the two-up-two-down cottage she sat in leisure
moments on a rickety chair at the front door gossiping across
the narrow street with neighbours. She sits on the same chair
now.

'But the view's different, see? You can keep an eye on the
river, see? A chap from the council said to me, "You've got a
fine prospect of the river here, Mrs Rockett." He was trying
to smooth me over, see, thinking I was going to crack on about
being on the fifth floor. I didn't say I liked it, didn't say I
didn't. Keep your mouth shut with chaps from the council,
that's best. You never know : they might give you a cut in the
rent, thinking you're going to crack on about something. But
he didn't, and I didn't. Never told him I was pleased as Punch,
being up here, keeping an eye on the river. It's all right, I tell
you. You use a bit of imagination, you can make out you can
see the whole bleedin' river—right up to the quiet part where
it begins. Gloucestershire, is it?'

'That's right,' I told her.

'Yes. Well, you can kid yourself you've got a pair of those
field glasses and can stretch your sight out, see the whole thing
end to end.' After a pause during which, I like to think, she
did just that, she added : 'I've been down to the end, the
mouth—the Nore, they call it. There's a lightship there and
you can't tell the river's any different to the sea, it's that wide.
That's the end of it—a great gaping mouth.' She reflected
again. 'Ugly, I suppose you'd call it, all this bit down this part,
London, with all the shit and muck. But it looks all right sometimes, you get a bit of sun on it. It's a good river.'

Mrs Rockett's husband, Albert, the waiter at the Café
Royal, was drowned in the good river on the night of the 6th
of January 1928. He had been on the late shift—the one that
included lunch, tea, dinner, and supper, as distinct from the
early one, which ran from breakfast to dinner—and left the
restaurant at one a.m.

'I know that, because I went up there after and saw the Mater dee Hotel. "Your Albert left at one, Mrs Rockett," he told me. "I think he'd had a fairly good day with his tips," he said, "and he might have thought of picking up a taxi round the back in Brewer Street, it being such a wild night." Well, he might at that. Albert never worried much about a bit of extravagance if he was in the money. He gave me a brooch once, having had a good dropsy from a party of eight who all got pissed on champagne. Me—a brooch! I never had no more'n a safety-pin in me life. I've got it now, in the box with his war medals. I look at it sometimes.

'So he might have got a taxi. But the bastard old river was up an' all round the West India Dock Road was flooded. So the cabby might've dropped him up the end of Commercial Road. We was flooded at home in the downstairs, the sticks floating about and the old cat swimming. I picked her up out of it and took her upstairs. Right angry she was and I dried her up a bit with some old newspapers. I looked out the window and hollered out—everybody was poking outa their upstairs and shouting it was a bloody fine kettle and saying about Noah's Ark an' that, an' I hollered back an' said they'd better get the bleeding lifeboat out. A bit crotchety, I was, with the kids keep asking if they could go down and paddle. "Paddle," I told 'em, "you'll get paddle acrost your arses if you don't lay down and wait till the old pot-and-pan comes home." "Old Man River", they kept singing, which was a song that was on the go at the time.

'The old man never did come home, of course. "Sunnink's kept 'im up there at the caffy," I thought when I could hear meself think, which wasn't offen with this weather going on. What with the wind an' the rain and the river bashing over the banks in bloody great waves because of this tidal wave, whatever it was, down the Nore, you got cross-eared with the noise. Never believe, looking down at it now, it'd ever stir itself up like that, would you? But I kept saying to meself it'd be all right. Three years we'd bin married then an' I'd be twenty-nine, Albert thirty. One of the kids was five, the other seven,

and the tiddler two—she'd bin born after we was married,
see. That was a mistake—musta bin.

'Well, I might keep telling meself it was all right, but I
wasn't so sure. Then a coupla the river cops come up the
street with lamps and wearing long boots like fishermen.
They'd got one o' those trumpet things you keep shouting
through at people with, like at the boat race.'

'A megaphone?' I said, fussily pressing for irrelevant
accuracy.

'I don't know. If you say so. I don't think I ever rightly
knew what they was called. But I knew what that cop was
calling through it, all right. "Rockett" he was calling. It said
in the papers there was fourteen people drowned that night.
Albert was the first, though. They'd found him floating down
Narrow Street. Nobody could tell me more than that. Never
did know what happened. The cops brought a rowing boat up
an' took me where they'd got him laid out. Some hall, it was.
We took the kids an' the cat too. They didn't want to do no
bleedin' paddling when they saw their old man laid out, I
tell you. Some doctor had to give 'em a pill or they'd've gone
on yelling all night. "He's hurt isself," they kept saying, when
you could hear what they was saying at all. He looked mucky
all right—slime all over. "Sod the Thames," I said.'

She paused and folded her arms. This gave her an em-
battled look; but it lasted only a moment. The arms were
unfolded and a hand put on each heavy knee.

'But I never used to say it during the war,' she went on.
'We used to go down the shelters to sleep, the kids and me,
when you could get any sleep. Wapping Underground—that
was my station. I got drawn by that sculpture, Henry Moore,
he made a piccher of me. Under the river that line runs, and
we used to say if Hitler dropped his shit there we'd get
drowned before we'd got time to fart bubbles up at 'im. It
wasn't in the cards for me to get drowned too, though. I s'pose
one was enough in one family. I used to lay there and think
of the old river over the top and feel right matey about it.
Well, it's wide there, and deep, and might've bounced the

buggers back, or sunnink. Comforting, you might say. Funny thing to think when your old man's been drowned in it, but there you are. They offered me to move away up to Bromley when the new building came after the war. Prefabs. But I said I'd sooner stay and keep an eye on the river. So they said I'd have to wait, an' I waited. I've got me patience, same as me health and strength, and there wasn't no hurry. I went and moved over the river to Deptford, near the gas works. There's another river runs in there—the Ravensbourne—and it suited me. I got a room there and a few of me sticks, and I could walk along past Greenwich Hospital to the cemetery and back through the park. I never minded walking. But I like the river best. Been on it a few times, I have. Down to Southend on day trips, up to Kingston and Hampton Court, where the maze is and all those picchers, up and down many a time. One of the first things I done when they built that exhibition after the war—Festival of Britain, they called it—was to go on the water buses. That was a good exhibition, that was. It told you about things—how we like the seaside and all water, and about the stars an' all that. Not much about the river. But I suppose they needn't because it was there. You writing a book about it, are you?'

I told her I was.

'Well, the best thing I ever see on that Thames was Churchill's funeral. I went up west to see 'im laid out. Candles, Dukes—the lot. All round him. I thought of the old begger laying in his box there—cigar an' all, I shouldn't be surprised. And 'is missis, when the day of the funeral came round. All over black, she was. Well, I could feel for her. You get stuck to a bloke after all those years, you must do. I couldn't help thinking of Albert—in the first war, he was, just about, along with Churchill in a way of speaking. It was a good funeral and it was right it should be—what he done for the country. The bit I likes best was when they carted him off Tower Pier and on to the boat. They say they hadn't done a funeral like this since Nelson's. All the music stopped when they put him aboard the boat—there was just some whistles, those navy

things they have for admirals and that—pipes, is it? And off
he went in the boat with the other boats after—his missis and
all the bigwigs. That's the best thing I ever see on the Thames.
It got everything wound up together. I mean, what everything means. . . .' She made a small gesture of inarticulate
resignation, raising both hands from her knees and spreading
them. 'I said to meself, "That's it, mate, you'll be all right.
You're on the right river".'

Bibliography

This was intended to be a work of informative entertainment rather than of scholarship; and although there are hundreds of books about the Thames I ignored all of them that seemed to be guided tours ('On our left now appears a fine eighteenth-century house . . .'), for I cannot compete with them. That left the specialised works, some of which I found very useful—for example, Hilaire Belloc's *Historic Thames,* Macdonald Hastings's *A Glimpse of Arcadia,* Henry Robinson's *Past and Present Conditions of the River Thames,* David Morley's *The London Water Supply,* and William Dugdale's *The History of Imbanking.*

The *Papers of the Geological Survey* gave me much of what I wanted about land formation.

For history I used for the most part the *Cambridge Medieval History,* the *Anglo-Saxon Chronicles,* the 1236 *Chronicle of Matthew Paris,* Stow's *History,* G. M. Trevelyan's *History of England* and *English Social History,* Lewis Mumford's *The City in History,* and the indefatigable diarists Pepys, Evelyn, and Celia Fiennes. County and town histories and the files of local newspapers yielded up more information than I could use in a thousand books. The stories about historical personages in the book I found either complete or piecemeal in standard biographies and autobiographies.

The Public Record Office enabled me to check a great many names, dates, and other facts. And the British Museum and the London Library filled in the gaps with broadsheets, pamphlets, and collections of esoteric papers.

Index

HERTF

BUCKINGHAMSHIRE

MARLOW

BISHAM

MAIDENHEAD

M

Windsor Race Course

CASTLE

WINDSOR

Windsor Great Park

STAINES

Kempton

BERKSHIRE

EGHAM

CHERTSEY

S U

WEYBRIDG

leoV